My Rough Diamond

My Rough Diamond

Doris Lemon

Marshalls

Marshalls Paperbacks
Marshall Morgan & Scott

3 Beggarwood Lane, Basingstoke, Hants

ISBN: 0 551 00957 8

Printed in Great Britain by
Hunt Barnard Printing Ltd., Aylesbury, Bucks.

To my children
June, Joyce and John

Contents

Foreword

I count it an honour to be asked to write a foreword to
this book by Doris Lemon telling the story of her 'rough
diamond' from her own experience of their life together.
They both have a special place in my heart which has
deepened into an enduring friendship.

It was in 1952 that I first became a minister to Fred
and his family at the Methodist Central Hall,
Southampton. Fred had just been released from
Dartmoor prison and had come straight to Southampton to be reunited to his wife and children. Joe
Blinco, my predecessor, had arranged for their
accommodation and a job for Fred to go to, and they
were busy in those first few weeks adjusting themselves
to their new and exciting situation. Then followed years
of testing and growing in grace, and, ultimately, the
emergence of Fred's ministry which is reflected in his
books – a special and unique ministry filled with an
understanding love to men and boys who have lost their
liberty, as well as their self-respect and their confidence.

During the years one is aware of another person who
proves to be a constant and potent factor in the story. It
is Doris – a most loyal and loving wife. Always Doris
is there, sharing in the trials and triumphs of a
progressive discipleship – always practical and down-
to-earth – often manifesting a divine gift of discern-

ment, as Fred explains on page 59 of *Going Straight*.

So now Doris has told her own side of the story with its ministry of encouragement, revealing what it is like to live with a (one-time) violent criminal changed into a gentle, considerate husband, and an old cockney barrow boy transformed into an eloquent and inspired preacher of the Gospel. Doris is telling the story of an amazing modern miracle. Paul sums it up in II Cor.5; 17, 'If anyone is in Christ, he is a new creation; the old has gone, the new has come!'

CHARLES J. CLARKE

Introduction

He performs wonders that cannot be fathomed Job 5:9

I am the wife of Fred Lemon. That is how I introduce myself because that is why I am writing this book. Also, that's how people usually think of me: as the wife of that man who was a convict and so nearly a murderer before he became a Christian – of all things! And Fred is quite well known these days, through his books, and because of the extensive preaching he does all over the country.

My husband has a wonderful testimony to the goodness of God, and to the change that can take place in anyone's life if he will give himself over to Christ. God has worked miracles in Fred's life, transforming him from a vicious, drunken, professional thief who nearly murdered a man, to the busy evangelist that he is today. But over the last few years many different people have approached Fred, after reading his books *Breakout* and *Going Straight*, (and now *Breakthrough*!) and said something like this; 'What a wonderful testimony you've got! The things that have happened to you! But what about Doris, your wife? Living with you for the last forty years! I bet she could say a thing or two! Why doesn't she write a book, telling her side of the story?'

After hearing this many times Fred came home one night and said to me: 'Doris, you're going to write a book. People want to hear your story.'

Now I live a very peaceful life which I enjoy very much. So I stared up at him over my knitting in astonishment.

'No, Fred, I am *not* going to write a book,' I said firmly. 'We've had quite enough publicity with you in the family.' And I went off to get supper.

But Fred is a persistent man, and although he didn't come and argue right away (and so delay supper, of which he is very fond), he kept mentioning it over the next few months.

'Think of all you've been through, living with me,' he'd say. 'I've been terrible to live with. You've had horrible things happen to you. You've been through almost every problem under the sun.'

'Yes,' I said thoughtfully, eyeing him and thinking back over the last forty years. Even now, I can hardly believe I've survived.

'Well, what a terrific story!' he said, his eyes shining.

I raised my eyebrows and sniffed. I felt the author in him was getting a bit carried away.

'What a rough marriage,' I replied.

'But think of all you've got to say!' he persisted.

'Fred, I would rather have had a more peaceful marriage and no story at all,' I said quietly.

But then I felt sorry I'd said that, for I think it hurt his feelings. 'I'm sorry I moaned,' I said, bringing in two mugs of tea from the kitchen. 'You've made me very happy in the last thirty years or so, and I'm just glad it's come out okay in the end.'

'Does that mean you'll do the book?' he said innocently, stroking the cat.

Ummm.

So I began to consider it. But I still had a lot of objections. Good ones, too.

'What exactly would I say?' I wondered one afternoon as I watched him weed the garden. 'I couldn't just tell my story.'

'Why not?' he demanded, sitting back on his heels and squinting at the tomatoes.

'Because my story is your story – I mean, we lived together. I can't just repeat the basic facts – how we married during the war, how we hardly knew each other, that we lived in Barking, that you were a thief but I didn't know, that we had three children, that you went to prison, that we then both went to prison ...'

I stopped to catch my breath. Reeling off one's life story in thirty seconds just isn't possible. '... How you became a Christian, how you changed in Dartmoor, how our marriage didn't break up, how Joe Blinko brought us to Southampton, how we adopted those five kids ... how we started the shop, entertained all those down and outs ...'

'Doris,' Fred interrupted, 'you don't have to tell *me* our life story, I do know it!'

'That's just my point!' I said triumphantly, holding the basket as he carefully picked some of the riper tomatoes for our tea-time salad. 'People already know our life story – they wouldn't want to hear the same thing from me all over again.'

'Why would it have to be all over again?' Fred stretched an aching back and glared at the cat, who was sniffing around some very young plants further down the garden.

'Fred,' I said patiently, 'Nobody would be able to care less about my life story if it wasn't for you. You're the interesting one, and what made *Breakout* so gripping is that you were the one doing all those terrible things – and yet still God was able to reach you. I was simply a young woman who married you and so got caught up in it all. So no one would bother to read anything I've got to say, unless they'd read all about you. It's *your* story. What could I add?'

'But surely you had some thoughts on it,' Fred urged, taking the basket from me as we walked back into the house.

'On what, our marriage?'

'Yes. On what it was like to be married to me, whether you found it difficult, why you didn't divorce me.'

'I've had plenty of thoughts on all that!' I exclaimed, looking up at his broad back in astonishment. Did he think I've just stayed around all these years because it has never occurred to me to go? I congratulate myself quite often that we are still together at all. If I hadn't learned God's way how to survive a difficult marriage, how to bring up children in the midst of it, and how to forgive and determinedly start again, I wouldn't be here right now.

'Well, there you are.' We reached the kitchen and Fred set down the basket. The late afternoon sun flooded through our window and lit up his face. 'You say that I'm the interesting one. So don't talk about my *story*, I've done that.' He grinned. 'Talk about *me*.'

My rough diamond. My lovable, kind, generous, aggravating, impossible, wonderful husband. Sometimes I want to hug him. Sometimes I could shake him. And all the time I don't know what I'd do without him.

So – here's the book about what I did *with* him,

instead. And he's taken some coping with, believe me! What's that old cliché – 'can't live with him, can't live without him'? That might have been written by me with Fred in mind!

1. *You fall in love with the strangest people…*

Wait, my daughter, until you find out what happens.
Ruth 3:18

You don't have to know a man all that well to fall in love with him. It's how we women break our hearts all the time.

Before the Second World War I was one of the thousands of young women from poor families in the East End of London trying to earn my living in London. I'd gone into a starch factory straight from school at fourteen and had hated the smell and the noise. I was fortunate enough to be able to change jobs, and by the time the hostilities with Germany began, was working at a furriers near Regent's Street.

I was an only child, but had several friends, and met many young men at the neighbourhood dances and social occasions. By rights I should have married one and settled down to be the wife of a shopkeeper or factory foreman. A humble but happy existence in the respectacle end of the working class of East London.

Instead, I married a soldier five years older than me whom I scarcely knew, a heavy drinker with a vile temper who was already an accomplished thief. A most unlikely choice! In later years my mother used to wonder dismally why I'd married such a man. I didn't. *I* knew perfectly well. I'd married him because I'd loved him.

When I look back on it all now, the only thing that Fred and I actually had in common was that we both came from the East End of London and were both poor. He was not only older, and from a different sort of family altogether, he'd also been away in India for the past five years with the army. Another difference was that I'd been raised to believe and trust in God. One of my earliest answers to prayer came when I was twelve – and I at last got a room, a little room all of my own.

All the differences make it amazing that the day we met we so much as noticed each other's existence!

Mind you, the atmosphere probably helped: it was at a wedding. My best friend Olive, with whom I'd grown up, was getting married to a long time sweetheart named Alf. When on the night before the wedding the best man fell ill, Fred, on the same ship just arrived back from India, was brought in as best man.

Olive and I had gone to school together, and since we'd left had continued to share the happy events of each passing season. The furriers I joined was fairly near where Olive worked, so we went on seeing each other. Then I discovered an amateur dramatics club nearby, decided that was where my glittering future lay, and joined in a flash. To my bitter disappointment, Olive could not be persuaded to join as well; but loyal friend that she was, she came along to see me play in such thrilling roles as one of the supportive 'maids' in *The Maid of the Mountain*.

Olive worked in service, for a Lord somebody or other who lived on Baker Street. While I preferred the commercial glamour of my job (we once made a fur coat for Gracie Fields that cost £4,000 even then!), I had to admit that her job had some perks; for when her Lord spent weekends in the country, and the butler was away, she was asked to stay and 'babysit' the house – and I was allowed to come and 'babysit' her.

It gave us a good opportunity to discuss Alf, a young man Olive had somehow found time to meet, fall in love with and become engaged to (perhaps during my absent hours rehearsing with the other maids on our indoor mountain?). They were going to marry as soon as he returned from India.

Olive was an orphan and had grown up in an institution – so what with no parents around and her fiancé in a ship off on the high seas, she and I went ahead and planned the entire wedding – it was taken for granted that I was the bridesmaid.

It was a lot of work – but in the end we'd got it just the way we wanted it – dresses, reception, everything (and I must say I can see the advantages of having the groom kept right away from the scene altogether – and just brought on with his best man in their suits on the day itself!).

And then – practically the night before the wedding, that wretched best man, a friend of Alf's in London, fell ill. It not only upset our plans for the wedding – it was to change my entire life.

For as bridesmaid, I was all dressed up that day, and my long fair curls and blue dress, Fred has since told me, bewitched him. I guess that romance was in the air and that he was highly susceptible to the gentler things of life – being just off an army ship. He was also a bit bored by the wedding ... anyway, he began to fall in love at once. He couldn't take his hangover-weary eyes (he'd been up celebrating the night before) off me. I sort of shimmered before him.

As a bridesmaid, of course, I was far too busy with the wedding itself, to worry much about some stand-in best man, beyond noticing that for some unfathomable reason he was making himself very pleasant indeed to my mother – they were nattering away like old chums. Being a naive type, I wasn't suspicious! Not even that night when my mother mentioned it.

'That Fred Lemon's a nice lad,' was her verdict as we sat at home, easing weary feet, and discussing the day. 'He's been a soldier in India for the last five years or so – that's where he met Alf. But he comes from East London – Barking. Very pleasant to talk to. You should have come over and met him.'

'Too late now,' I laughed, in my ignorance.

For on Monday a small, humble card arrived on our doorstep, addressed to me. Fred Lemon would like to meet me at Fenchurch St. Station that evening.

I was astonished, and showed it to Mum.

'Oh Doris, why not? He's really very nice.'

'Well, all right, but I'll have to hurry, I was late getting in from work today.' A glance in the mirror reassured me that a lot of my special hair-do still remained.

So I set off. And if you think Fenchurch St. Station is hardly an auspicious place to meet to begin a romance, I couldn't agree more! But the main snag was that it absolutely poured with rain – not only reducing my hair to stringy rat's tails, but putting an end to Fred's shy suggestion of a walk. Instead, we huddled together under the bleak, windy arches of the station. I noticed Fred was looking rather forlorn. 'Come on,' I said firmly. 'We can't stay here. I'll take you back to my home. We can talk to my mum.'

The evening was a success. Mum was delighted and pulled up a couple of kitchen chairs for us both at our large kitchen table. She and Fred talked away about the war and his life in India, for I was content just to listen. Just as well – I doubt I would have got a word in edgeways anyway!

Fred was very friendly and a great talker. He was also old-fashioned polite. I certainly didn't guess how much the evening meant to him until I heard a few days later that he'd taken lodgings nearby. I was surprised and touched – I'd still thought our first date was out of friendliness, and would be the last I'd see of him.

And so we became friends. I liked him. Very much! He was different from the other boys I'd met, and I felt attracted by the unfamiliar. For one thing, he was that bit older, and had seen a lot of life at twenty-six. I felt comfortable with him, it was no effort talking to him at all. We grew closer, which suited me fine. During our dating, if I saw him once a month, I was lucky. The war kept our soldiers very busy. As he came and went, I thought about him a lot. Only a few things caused me a second thought, a puzzled moment or two.

One of these was meeting his mother, who invited us to tea late one afternoon. She welcomed me in the unmistakable accents of a true Cockney at the front door of her little house in Barking. While she got some soup ready, I glanced about me and liked what I saw. It was much like my home, with its neatness and comforting atmosphere. But although Mrs Lemon was friendly as we chatted, I could see that she really didn't seem to know Fred all that well, or to care at all about what he did.

But what surprised me most was that Fred didn't notice *my* surprise, and seemed unaware that everything wasn't quite what it should be. And because I was already so drawn to him, perhaps this aroused my

21

sympathy even more – a feeling which in women can lead so easily to love. That this had been the kind of place he called 'home' and had wanted to flee to from those horrid state institutions he'd grown up in, really opened my eyes to what his background must have been like – more so than any hard luck talk he could have given me!

Not that he's ever been the self-pitying kind, though goodness knows he'd had some very rough knocks in childhood. Fred was one of eleven children. He'd been sent away to a children's home when only five or six, when, for several reasons his mother was unable to care for him, and, because of a very rebellious nature, had been under the strong arm of discipline ever since – from schools to the harsher measures taken by the army. But though he'd brought much on himself, I couldn't help having sympathy for a youngster who'd grown up without any parental care, love or guidance. I felt so sorry – and I realised how hard it must have been for him. After all, it was hard for most East End children before the war. It wasn't rare to see them wandering barefoot on even the coldest days, with most likely very little in their stomachs – and they were the ones with homes! But with no parents to care at all, it must have been awful. You had to be tough just to survive.

This I knew, but not in very much detail, for he wasn't one to talk much about his past. Was this why I didn't realise quite how much his past had affected him? On the way home that evening, I gathered he'd been glad to reach adulthood, and to be united with his family again after all those difficult times (little did I know then just *how* attached he was to his family). He was pleased with the way the day had gone, with the way in which his mother and I had got on. As for my own opinion? She seemed nice enough – and certainly, in her way, fond of Fred.

His father I never met. He had died in 1927 and his mother had remarried. His mum and stepfather fought quite a bit, as I was to find out when I got to know them better.

The second incident was the night Fred took me to a party at a friends' house in Barking. When we arrived I could hardly believe my eyes! Fifty or sixty people were all trying to jam themselves into a small terraced house. The guests were everywhere – on the stairs, in the garden, in the kitchen, upstairs. Fred sprang into the crowd with joyful cries of recognition. I followed, more slowly, feeling overwhelmed and tongue-tied. There was drinking and gambling, and an attempt at card tricks, until Fred set not only a pack of cards but also part of the floor on fire with one of his more complicated ideas. After that they went back to the drinking!

All in all, I didn't think much of the evening. But you know how it is when you're falling in love: anything in the man that troubles you, any bad habits or ways, you somehow don't blame on him. I suppose, having fallen in love *despite* them, you conclude that such ways aren't *really* him – that he's just the victim of a bad background, or circumstances. And perhaps when you look at him and love him, what you're really loving is an ideal version of your man, whom you're sure will slowly emerge from the chrysalis of his background.

The third incident was quite startling to my whole family. Our house in Bermondsey was at the end of a terraced row and had a low wall all around it. One afternoon when we were all out, Fred arrived with a pillow-case of sugar, packages of meat and other goodies he had stolen from the army. He jumped the wall, climbed in the window, and left it all on the table for my mother. When my mother got in and saw it, of course the first thing she said was, 'Here, Doris, where did all this stuff come from?' She wasn't stupid, she had a good idea, and Fred was surprised next time he saw her to find he had not made her good books.

To make things worse (poor Fred, he was never very lucky), he'd also left his gun by accident. My father found it and went into a tirade about 'any young man stupid enough to leave such a lethal weapon . . .' All the same, they soon forgave him, and appreciated his gesture for the way in which it had been meant. These were the war years, and petty thievery was rife. My parents recovered, and our relationship grew closer over the next few weeks. Well, as close as the Second World War would permit! Looking back, I wonder if the efforts to carry on normal relationships despite long absences led people to make some very poor judgments.

Absence makes young lovers more determined to be together, and absence with danger only increased the bond. As for anything slightly wrong that needed to be talked out, well, our world was in chaos – how do you think carefully about the finer points of your boyfriend's character when buildings are being bombed all around you? We didn't even dare go to movie houses for fear they'd be bombed and we'd be burned alive. Coming to see me once, Fred arrived just as the gas works at the bottom of our street was bombed. He was blown right down the street and I found him in the gutter with the skin off his face and hands.

He always came to me – it was too dangerous and difficult for me to get across London. As for his mates, who were the cause of so much future trouble, I hardly met them. Not even Fred wanted them around when he was courting!

I met him in the summer and by late autumn, though we'd only been together a handful of times, I knew that I was beginning to love this big, kindly, rather shy young man who appeared at infrequent intervals. I pitied what

I knew of his past, and admired him for having survived it. Perhaps had I been older and the times more sane, I would have realised that his rough good manners towards my mum and me were the result of formality. Fred had never cared for a woman before, and falling in love awed him as much as it did me. He was a bit shy, but eager to please me. It was totally unfamiliar territory for him, and as you often find with rough and ready men, love made him – during his courtship – kindness and sweetness itself.

Life was chaotic and uncertain: when we said good-bye to each other, I never knew when I was going to see him again – or even *if* I was going to see him again. Then Christmas, 1939, came, bringing a box of chocolates from Fred – and probably the most important decision I have ever made.

For the chocolate box wasn't as innocent as it looked. When I opened it up (at my mum's sweet-toothed request) a glittering ring fell out. In his character-istically unexpected way, Fred had proposed!

I turned the ring over and over in my hand, a warm glow of happiness replacing the incredulity. This was it then; my first boyfriend, my first proposal of marriage. What should I do?

I decided to accept and wrote telling him of my decision. I knew I loved Fred – his company was easy and natural, and he seemed the kind of man with whom I could lead a decent life. Perhaps if I'd been older, or more experienced I would have been wiser. I would have taken more seriously the great difference in our upbringing and the effect that it was bound to have on our outlook on life. Perhaps I didn't realise how blessed I'd been that both Mum and Dad were stable and God-fearing, and just took it for granted that my own marriage would turn out the same. But did I ever really believe that he would change completely into the amiable self he was when he visited me in Bermondsey?

Fred wrote back, somewhat shyly and stiffly. I understood. For all his bravado, he could be a shy man, and even stuttered at times. The wedding was set for August – just a year from the time I'd first met him.

2. First days – getting to know the man you've married

As I have observed, those who plough evil and those who sow trouble reap it. Job 4:8

I married Fred in August, 1940. It was a hectic day – we were so busy that the youngest of my four bridesmaids wore her dress back to front for the entire day and nobody even noticed until the pictures of the wedding came back from the photographers – all the buttons were down the front of her instead of the back. I wondered if my relatives had seen it and had wondered what kind of bride I was, not to have noticed such a thing on my own bridesmaid!

Fred had planned the wedding, and he rather overdid it in his enthusiasm. He arranged that the bridesmaids and I should be picked up in a taxi, and taken to the church in Barking. But instead of going straight to the church, he and his mates were so hilarious that they ordered the taxi to drive round and round Barking, beeping the horn loudly. I giggled and didn't mind at all, though I wondered just when, if ever, I was actually going to arrive at the church.

The ceremony, when we finally got there, was simple

but deeply meaningful to me. This was my wedding day! As the organ began I had a lump in my throat. I met Fred down at the front and I put his glassy stare down to the same nerves that were affecting me. I held his arm and took my vows to God and to him. My voice sounded very thin as I said, 'I, Doris, take you, Fred . . .'

I can look back on that service now with fondness, but that hasn't always been so. During the early years of my marriage it hurt me to think about it, for I'd found out that Fred was dead drunk and couldn't remember a word of the service. He and his mates had started celebrating early, long before the ceremony itself. Fortunately he hadn't reached the roaring drunk stage, and he still had some sense of occasion left. Every time the minister looked him in the eye and said something, Fred, solemn as an owl, repeated it. But today, he has only the haziest memory of any service taking place at all.

'I now pronounce you man and wife,' intoned the cleric. The wedding march rang forth a few minutes later, and we stepped into the sunshine outside for the photos. I heard Fred's mate shouting 'So where's the booze?' and a whole new way of life opened before me . . .

There is an old saying that if you've made an unwise choice in marriage, you at least have the wedding and the honeymoon before the unpleasant truth dawns. Not so with us. I realised something was pretty far wrong at the reception. My side of the family stood around nibbling cake (not knowing it was stolen) and sipping tea through lips that got tighter and tighter in shocked disapproval as Fred's family gleefully launched themselves into a drinking spree that was to last for three full days and nights. The first evening we were all at Fred's sister's house in Barking. Then, of course, many of the guests began to drift away – his sisters went home, my parents and relatives left. But some of Fred's friends just stayed on and on. I didn't know any of them and I hardly saw Fred at all. I went to bed when I could keep awake no longer, and when I came down the next morning, there were Fred and his mates, asleep over bottles.

I was a bit astonished and hurt – but reasoned that it was on account of the occasion, and that his sort of people always celebrated weddings like this. So I went to bed each night, though nobody else did. They just kept going, wandering from the downstairs room to the pub along the road and back again.

Finally on the third day, Fred and I left what remained of the party and made our way back to Peckham. My mother had kindly offered us a room in their small flat in which to set up our first home. She'd given me some furniture and I'd spent hours fixing it up. I was so glad to get there – despite the fact that Bermondsey was being more heavily bombed than Barking (we were near to Surrey Docks, and it was all afire).

Fred went back into the army, over to Larn in Ireland, and I went back to work. I missed him badly, but I was content. When I'd finally had him all to myself our times together had been marvellous. I loved him very much.

In the Bible it says that when a man marries, he should leave his mother and father, and should cleave to his wife, and the two become one. So no wonder the early years of our marriage were to prove disastrous! For you could not have found a greater contrast to what we actually did.

Of course, it is difficult to 'cleave' to your husband when he is away at war and you're living with your parents in their small flat, spending some nights at home, and others diving eighty-five feet down the Old Borough Street tube, praying that the bombs don't hit the floodgates and let the Thames in to drown you and your 7,000 companions.

I hardly saw Fred at that time, for his leaves from the army were few, and anyway, everyone's mind was taken up with the war. It was hard not to be, especially if you lived in Bermondsey. We were living near a relay station that apparently interested the Germans very much, for we were bombed and bombed and bombed. Many a night I spent on roofs with other women, pushing off unexploded incendiary bombs. And I have memories – horrible ones – of sights that will stay with me till I die.

We had a school right on our corner, and I was at home the day they bombed it. You don't recover easily from seeing a child walking in front of you one minute, and blown to the four winds the next. I saw them running, being machine gunned and dying in front of me. It was a living hell.

Those days are very confused for me now – just an endless cycle of running whenever the air raid sirens sounded, and creeping back up afterwards to try and deal with whatever new devastation the bombs had left.

As a family, we had other troubles as well. My father had been unwell for years, with something akin to a duodenal ulcer, and had many attacks. When that happened, his forehead would go all silver like a fish, and soon he would be vomiting blood. My mother and I tried in vain to get him to stop work as an engineering foreman in Tower Bridge Road; but surprisingly, the doctor disagreed with us. 'Anything that will take his mind off his pain, Doris,' he said to me. So Dad continued working, and fortunately, I was able to get a job at the same factory, and thus be near him, ready to be called by his work-mates whenever he had one of his turns. Though there was little we could do for him.

But, oddly enough, all this didn't hurt my marriage in the least. I was still very much in love with Fred, and eager to see him whenever I could. I looked forward to his coming home, and was so very happy in those brief days and nights I had him to myself. I held him in my arms and dreamed happily of the day when this terrible war would be over, and we would settle down somewhere in our own home. I didn't care how small or humble it was, it would be ours, somewhere we could start life together, and I could spend time with this man I'd married.

And all the time he was lying to me. For these 'one day' leaves which he spent with me, and at the end of which he would borrow some of my hard earned and barely spared money, were really no such thing. The army had not given him a day and a night off; it had given him a week. But he didn't want to spent it with me, and he'd be off to Barking for a booze-up with his family for the rest of his six days, leaving me with the impression he had gone back to his duties. But I never suspected what was going on.

So, ironically, it was when the fighting calmed down and Fred and I saw more of each other that the troubles began. We left Peckham and moved to Barking, to live in a room in his mother's house until we found a home of our own. We had the lower part of the house and I was eager to make the best of it. We managed to furnish it, put up curtains and add all the trimmings dear to my home-maker's heart. That new house did a tremendous amount to cheer me and make me believe we could have a home at last – for a while.

Yet I sometimes think that had we been somehow able to get away from Barking and his people, we would have had a far better chance of survival. Fred and I had seen so little of each other, we really needed to get reacquainted. But Fred neither recognised nor wanted this. I was his wife now, and he took our marriage totally for granted.

Emotionally and mentally, Fred had never left home. He was still his mother's son, his brothers' brother – their mate, their Fred. He has always had a very strong 'clannishness' and he saw himself as still a part of the Lemon family. He wasn't ready to become a husband, and as we settled into Barking, this became ever more apparent.

I didn't feel at home in Fred's mother's house, though I was grateful to her for letting us come. The first thing I noticed were the people – there were so many of them! Fred had nine brothers and sisters, and countless mates and acquaintances – the house was always teeming with people. At first they seemed just a mass of faces. After a few weeks they began to sort themselves into names and personalities, but even so, I could never remember all their names; and when I heard snatches of their conversation, I didn't think I was missing much by not improving our relationship.

My Freddie was a great one for being one of the gang, usually the ringleader. He was a born leader, and the others applauded his jokes and wild drinking. They found him a great companion.

To me he was no companion at all. I never saw him, especially after the first baby arrived. I felt lonely and betrayed. I could never get him on his own – if his mates had gone home, there was always the odd brother or sister hanging about. And with them around, he would never listen to me.

Usually after work he wasn't home at all. He'd be out, drinking with his brothers and mates. They'd have fights in the streets and afterwards come bursting into the house. 'Tolerance', I'd tell myself, biting back the reproaches, 'You've got no right to tell others how to live.' Or he'd come in drunk and in a filthy mood. 'Patience,' I'd say to myself, creeping round the bedroom so as not to rile him, 'He's had a difficult childhood and this is the only life he's ever known.'

But all the things he enjoyed and wanted in life were so different from mine that I despaired of ever fitting in. His family would have welcomed me I know. Even as it was, they took me along a couple of times down to their local pub. But at the pub there was nothing but drink, drink, drink and vulgar, pointless jokes. I was bored stiff. I tried not to show my disgust, I smiled wanly at the hilarity. I guess they thought me dull and witless – anyway, they soon ignored me. I would sit and watch Fred and wonder how he could be like this. He was a different person altogether from the one I had married. Surely he didn't really want this kind of life. Surely he loved me like he'd said he did and wanted to build a life together with me ... but he never did. I was expected to fit in the best I could.

But how could I fit in? I didn't even want to. His brothers and sisters and mother were unlike any family I'd ever met – they had rows openly in the street! They didn't 'interfere' with Fred and me – they didn't need to. There wasn't much left of a 'Fred and I' to talk about. If anything, it was 'Fred and them'. I didn't feel like a wife, but a chattel.

It's true, that old saying, that men marry women thinking they'll stay the same, and that women marry men thinking they'll change them. We seem to think that the tenderness and considerateness a man shows us during the engagement is how he will automatically treat us for the rest of our lives. We have a terrible desire to tame a man; women can be very selfish. We want to fall in love, we want a man to love us, we want to build a cosy home, we want him to be attentive to us. The emotional and idealistic importance that we set on our dreams is very great.

Men (at least Fred!) seem to enter marriage with much less thought. They love the woman, the woman is eager to please them, and according to their temperament, they enter the future jauntily, believing serenely in their competence to deal with problems. Many men are very materialistic, especially younger men. They want a house, then a better house, and better stuff to put in it. They think they've got the world figured out and that they're going to beat the system.

Of course, when differences began to show between us, I was the one who'd be left in tears; he'd be off down at the pub. His reaction to our rows was anger at first, and then he'd brush it off as me just being difficult.

But I found it shattering. In those days, being married meant your life was built around your husband. He was the most important person in my life, and to argue with him shattered me. In fact, during those early years, there were times I felt my marriage was so dead that the only decent thing to do would have been to bury it.

Meanwhile, my own parents got somewhat embroiled in the arguing. After the arrival of June, our first baby, our quarrelling had started in earnest. By this time we'd moved from his mother's to the house nearby. Unfortunately, we didn't have the house entirely to ourselves: a Dutch family rented part of the upstairs for some time, and at another point Fred's brother John and his wife, also named Doris (which caused considerable confusion at times!) had two rooms upstairs. I took to fleeing from the awful atmosphere of our Barking home to my parents in Peckham.

Sometimes I'd stay away for up to as much as a week at a time.

My parents were disgusted with Fred, and often wondered why on earth I'd ever married him – even though, for their sake, I told them as little as possible of what was going on over in Barking. Then, when we were expecting our second baby, and Fred was again away with the army, I even left Barking altogether for a time, and found myself a flat near Peckham, which I didn't let anyone tell Fred about. I was sick to death of him, and wanted some peace.

Eventually he traced me, and my mother found him one night sitting on the wall outside the house where my flat was. Never one to mince her words, she said, 'What are you doing here, Fred Lemon? I never did like you, and I don't like you now, and I never will like you. You either take care of my Doris, or get out and leave her alone.' Mother's furies were really quite something, and it was the first time that either of our parents had directly intervened between us. It sobered Fred down for a while, and we returned to Barking and some peace, if little happiness.

My parents had a talk with me as well. My father was worried. 'We're getting on, Doris, and neither of us are well (at this time my mother had cancer, and was dying, but we didn't yet realise it). 'You can't keep running back to us here in Peckham. You've got to stay and make a go of it.'

I kept trying, and used their home as a bolthole only when things really became impossible. For in a household where the step-father and mother are burning stolen tobacco outside the back door while the police are hammering on the front door, I saw little hope of anything ever changing.

Not that Fred's family were totally bad people. They

never treated me with anything but kindness – according to their lights. I realised this, appreciated it for how it was meant, and have always liked them for it. If I found their lifestyle very different, they must have felt just the same towards me; but never once did they ever try to persuade me to join in the constant heavy boozing, the boisterous talk and behaviour, the inevitable fights. In fact, in our different ways, we helped each other over the years, though there was never more than a limited amount of understanding or sympathy between us.

Whatever women look for in choosing a husband, no one could have made a more mistaken choice – as it seemed for years – than I had. I had looked for friendship, dependability, a man I could trust, with whom I could build a God-fearing, temperate home. I got a hard, callous drunkard who'd hardly talk to me, who was never there!

All the same, it wasn't all bad. There were some tender moments. I have memories of one night in particular when Fred showed me such compassion and understanding that I have never forgotten it. It was an awful night – London was being blitzed and the sirens wailed and wailed while bombs exploded only blocks from us. Suddenly I took it into my head that I must go home to my parents to see if they were all right.

'Oh Fred,' I whimpered as the planes droned over, clinging to him in terror. He detached himself gently and left to get my coat. 'Come on,' he said kindly, 'I'll take you home.' He picked up the baby and waited until I got ready.

I knew it was dangerous even as we closed the front door, but I was set on going. Even so I don't think I would have chanced it if I'd known how close the bombs were dropping. We passed the ends of roads where building after building was on fire. I clung to Fred and he carried June.

It took us hours and hours to get from Barking to Peckham like that, and by the time we got there it was almost dawn and the raid was long over. But Fred kept going, and I followed in grateful silence. How easily he could have said back in Barking. 'Doris, you're crazy, you'll just have to wait till morning.'

I loved him very much at times like that, and wished with all my heart that things could always be this gentle and understanding between us.

But of all those early years, the most terrible thing that happened to me was the death of my mother. It was a slow and painful death, and I cared for her at home though I had June and Joyce by that time. I travelled to Peckham a lot and nursed her as best I could. I knew she was seriously ill even when they let her out of hospital, but no one told me she had cancer, and I had no idea at all she'd been sent home to die. My father couldn't bring himself to tell me. One day she was in such a bad way that I took the chance of leaving the two little girls unattended with her at the flat and ran across the neighbourhood to get the doctor. 'Please come,' I gasped. 'My mother isn't getting better. In fact, today she looks awful, doctor, like she could die.'

I shall never forget the look on his face as he turned to me. 'But Doris,' he said 'she will never get better. Surely you know that?'

I stared at him, stunned.

'Do you mean to tell me your father hasn't told you?' he continued angrily. 'Doris, your mother is dying, there is nothing we can do.'

She died next day in my arms. The shock of it left a terrible scar on me and even all these years later I flinch at the memory. Mother died at the height of the rows between Fred and me. For years I questioned God about that. Why did He let her die just when I needed her most? It was hard, terribly hard. Sometimes even now I sit and think about it all. What would those years have been like if she'd been well, if she'd been someone I could turn to and depend on? I needed *help*, I was married to a downright rotter!

3. *Booze, booze, booze*

Who has woe? Who has sorrow? Who has strife? Who has complaints? . . . Who has bloodshot eyes? Those who linger over wine . . . Proverbs 23:29, 30

Nowadays, when Fred cries out 'What about a drink?' as he's watching the sport on T.V., there's no question of a misunderstanding between us. I bustle around to get the kettle on, and sort out the mugs with the tea bags. I suppose we drink gallons of the stuff. Except for the occasional cup of coffee, tea's the strongest brew he's drunk for years. I gladly get it for him whenever and wherever he suddenly feels the need for it, for since, with God's help, he's cut out the strong stuff, I've no longer despised him. As I did once . . .

Fred was drunk the day I married him and he stayed that way for years. He swam in booze. He stank of it. And as it made him angry and violent, it very nearly ended our marriage. For nothing drives a woman to despair quicker than when she sees her husband doing something foolish and wrong, and knows she has no control over him, no ability to stop him. It's frightening.

That's what it's like to be married to a heavy drinker. Fred drank himself paralytic during the early years of our marriage, despite all my protests. In fact, he deeply resented me trying to get him to stop, while I came to hate the very sight of him staggering home every night. Life was bleak and uncertain, filled with vicious rows that would start at the point my distress turned to anger. Though I remember one night when Fred was too drunk to quarrel ...

He and some friends had come in from our local pub in Barking, and he was so plastered he couldn't even speak. He sank into an easy chair, his eyes glassy, his face flushed. Suddenly, I went beserk. Anyone as drunk as that didn't deserve to be conscious!

I snatched up a nearby ornament and struck him furiously over the head. He slumped and was out – cold. His friends thought this was hysterically funny and they rolled about, whooping with laughter. I left the room in disgust, having for once had the last word where Freddie Lemon was concerned.

My victory was a private one: when he came round a while later, he'd no idea I'd even hit him! In fact, I'm not sure whether or not he even realised he'd been unconscious. When you're that drunk, the line between consciousness and unconsciousness wavers a lot! Any headache that followed I suppose he put down to a well-earned hangover.

Of course, a wife can't simply brain her husband every time he returns from the pub: to say nothing of the strain on his skull, it doesn't improve your marriage. Also, and most important, it doesn't begin to solve the problem! And, of course, I knew that full well even as I brought the ornament into violent contact with the back of his head. But if you've ever been involved with someone who drinks, you'll well understand the tremendous anger and frustration that built up inside me.

For what possible solution *is* there? He likes his booze, and nothing and no one is going to stop him from having it. And if you think he's odious and awful when he's been drinking, just try pleading with him to stop, or try and prevent him from going to the pub! The reaction you get doesn't bear thinking about!

With Freddie, booze was one of the great joys of life. And unless he himself had been changed on the inside, by God, no outward pressures would have been able to make him decide to stop. When we first married, I wouldn't have minded him having his evening 'pint' – for I knew he wasn't like me – a confirmed teetotaller. We'd been brought up differently, and I didn't see why I should bulldoze him into living as I saw fit. After all, he never tried to get me to drink. In my innocence, I saw no problem ahead.

But Fred devoted all his free time, energy (and a great deal of our money) to pickling himself at our local boozer. In the early days, he persuaded me to come along to be sociable. But I hated it and took to waiting for him outside, or better yet, staying at home altogether. I'd sit alone and knit after washing up the tea-things; Freddie would have dropped in for a quick bite on his way to join his mother, brothers and step-father in the pub.

I was very lonely. I detested the reek of alcohol that clung to him, and the evil tongue and temper it inspired. It dawned on me – painfully – that as far as Fred was concerned, love of booze came before love of me. Hurt, bewilderment, anxiety, tears, all followed one another rapidly. He didn't care. But did he realise he'd damaged to the core my love and admiration for him? They gradually seeped away, leaving only disillusionment and a growing indifference towards him. I withdrew into myself, and cared for our children. If he'd harmed one hair of their heads while drunk I'd have killed him, but otherwise, I got to the point where, if he wanted to lie in the gutters, I just let him. I found him once lying unconscious below a barrel of beer with it trickling down his throat. This was my husband. I felt so angry, so hateful, that it frightened me.

His excess was really something to be marvelled at. I remember the time he and his mates had experimented and came up with an alcoholic concoction of which a single glassful would lay each one flat out on the carpet. After watching in amazement as one man after another went over like a felled oak, I withdrew. If they enjoyed that, they and that brew deserved each other. Fred loved it, and gulped down as much as he could before he passed out.

Looking back, my disgust at what he did and how vile and despicable drink made him are no less – but I can now pity him too. He came from a background where excessive drinking was the norm, not the exception. Also, he lived through a war where 'leaves' from the army quickly became drinking jamborees for thousands of tired, strained soldiers ... why *should* he have been any different?

Fred needed his motive in life changed – help which was beyond me to give. In those days I was too discouraged and bewildered to live out my childhood faith. I seldom prayed, and though my belief in God was always strong, He seemed very far away.

But He wasn't, and I was to learn how great is His power and grace towards those that ask for it. For after his experience with God in prison, Fred at last agreed with the writer in Proverbs that much drinking is 'not wise'! And to my delight (and slight incredulity) he chose sobriety – and me.

You can imagine my deep contentment when I tell you now that my Freddie hasn't boozed for years. I can't begin to say what a difference it has made to our marriage and to my love for him, so let me put it a different way: if he had gone back to boozing after his release from Dartmoor, I would have left him. Not only had I had enough – it's no atmosphere in which to raise children.

One incident, soon after he left prison, which showed me how much God had come to mean to him was when he had been feeling restless one afternoon and had gone into a pub for a single pint. A Christian he knew found him coming out and told him sternly that if he wanted to be a Christian, he couldn't drink at *all*.

Whether or not every Christian would accept such a harsh verdict I doubt – but it cut Freddie to the quick, and that was the last time he went to a pub. Because he had found God's love for him, somehow the drinking and the old ways didn't seem so attractive any more. And that, believe me, is a miracle!

4. Please stop –
you'll strangle me soon

... The unfaithful have a craving for violence.
Proverbs 13:2

Fred's arms have made me ache all my life. But nowadays – and indeed for the past thirty years – it's a nice ache. When I see him stretch out those great hands of his, I quickly put down whatever it is I'm holding: no plate or tea cup has a chance of surviving one of those special bearhugs of his. If he's feeling in an exceptionally affectionate mood and hugs me tightly, I can literally ache for days afterwards.

But Fred has been reaching out for me ever since I married him, and it used to terrify me. For in the early days of our marriage the aches were anything but nice ...

There are some things about Fred which I would like to forget. They're very painful to remember, even now. Which makes this a very hard chapter to write: there's no joy in recalling the beatings he once gave me, the hard slaps around the face, the violent shoves (one which sent me straight across a dining room table – to crash painfully on the other side). And worst of all, the three separate occasions he went completely beserk and tried to strangle me.

No, I don't like remembering, but I can't forget. And the only reason I'm still with him is because, with God's help, I've been able to forgive. But it hasn't been easy. Any woman with a violent husband will know just what I mean.

It began very early in our marriage, and actually I don't entirely blame Fred. I didn't even wholly blame him at the time. What can you expect of a man whose family has brawls – with knives – in the street in the middle of the night?

One erupted shortly after we moved to Barking to live with his mother. He and his brothers and sisters and some mates had all been drinking heavily when suddenly, about midnight, I heard shouting and the slamming of doors downstairs (I was on my way to bed). I'd already had private doubts as to some of the guests, so I rushed down to find out what on earth was going on.

The living room was empty, cigarette smoke hanging in the fuggy air. But the front door was open, and I heard shouts and pounding feet out in the street. I went to the door and stared, aghast. Before me was a group of men, fighting and kicking, while shadowy figures flitted to and fro on the fringe. Fred may or may not have started it, but he was certainly in the thick of it.

Other neighbours had opened their doors, and by the lights I suddenly spotted one man unsheath a knife ...

Fred's brother! He was going to stab Fred's brother!

I'm small and skinny but I didn't think twice. I flung myself on the man, grabbing at his arm, weighing him down for those few precious seconds while the others wrestled the knife from him.

If I expected congratulations for my swift action, I was disappointed. Instead, a woman loomed up out of the darkness and attacked me, getting in a few sharp kicks and scratches before I could grasp what was happening.

'You -----!' she shrieked, and slowly I understood: she'd *wanted* Fred's brother to be stabbed! I'd never done anything violent in my life, but I had to now. We screamed and tore at each other (amazing how strong the instinct for self-preservation is!).

Afterwards, when I'd collapsed in the safety of my home, the shock hit me. What kind of neighbourhood was this? I'd never seen anything like it; it seemed evil to me, and I hated it. I surveyed my bruised face and torn clothes and couldn't stop sobbing.

Drinking. That, of course, was the root of the whole problem. Fred's family swam in booze – and drinking made everybody so violent! Certainly it brought out Fred's hot temper – which time and again ended in blows. And as he was usually mad at me for one thing or another (and I don't pretend I didn't deserve it sometimes), I bore the brunt of it.

The first evening that he came home and lashed out at me with those great fists of his, I thought I would choke on my fear. The pain of being struck (and don't let anyone kid you with theories of how it's not the pain that hurts so much as the shock!) – as well as the emotional anguish, crushed me for days. A great psychological divide had been crossed – my husband, whom I loved, had treated me the way he would a dog with whom he was angry. He had used his far greater strength deliberately to hurt me.

Things could never be the same again. I'd lost my trust in him.

After that, it was a miserable mixture of going canny with him, trying not to irritate him (almost anything did that), and fighting back when I couldn't bear the things he said and did any longer. This went on for several years; how did either of us cope?

The most amazing, even absurd incidents stand out in my mind. And when I glance out my kitchen window today and see Fred quietly pottering in the garden, tying up his tomato plants, it seems incredible that he and I should ever have behaved so. Ludicrous, almost. Yet appalling at the time.

Like the night of the scissors ...

Fred had had some of his mates over and one of their wives had been teasing him. Fred was not known in those days for his ability to laugh at himself, and was in a seething fury with just enough self-restraint left not to explode.

I'd gone to our bedroom and sat down on the edge of our bed, wondering if his guests were going soon and if it would be very rude of me to go on to bed anyway. When he strode into the room, flushed and breathing hard, I was startled.

He stared down at me, cursing under his breath, and suddenly lunged for me, swiping at both sides of my face with his hands. The slaps were hard, and would have loosened some teeth, or left me bruised and in pain for days. Had they landed. But they didn't because, in desperate self-defence, I snatched up a pair of sharp sewing scissors that lay on my bed-side table and stabbed them at his upper thigh.

Fred jumped back just in time. I was bitterly disappointed to have missed. He slunk out of the room and I cursed myself for not being quicker. And to show you just how far violence had affected me, I didn't stop and reflect on the tragic situation of a wife feeling regret because she's not been able to plunge a pair of sharp scissors up to their hilt into her husband's thigh.

He never attacked me sadistically, stone sober. And

he *never* touched the children. He wasn't calculatingly cruel – his violence was a result of drink on top of a vicious temper and an unhappy relationship with me that caused us both a lot of frustration. I became his victim because he was already angry with me.

But for several years I reasoned that as long as I kept out of the way when he was really angry, I was fairly safe. Only I wasn't. For Fred's first attempt at strangling me came at the most unlikely time imaginable.

Nowadays I am a very sound sleeper (Fred says burglars could carry off our entire household – including our bed, with me in it, and I'd never know it) – and in those days I was pretty relaxed in bed too. But though along with all wives I'd learned to expect interruption from my husband if I went to bed first (from 'Where are my pyjamas?' to him discovering with his bare foot the sharp pointed brooch I hadn't realised had come off my dress and dropped to the carpet) I do and always have maintained that no woman should wake up in alarm when she hears her husband coming to bed. And certainly, until that night, I never had. After all, if you're asleep, how can you find yourself in the middle of an argument?

But things had been bad between us for a long time. He knew I despised his drinking, and one night when he came to bed, my peaceful sleeping must have seemed to him to mock everything he did and stood for. Anger that had been simmering within him for days suddenly exploded.

The first I knew was when he leaped on the bed astride me and groped for my throat. I woke and gasped as his fingers began to squeeze and wring. Fred's face was livid with drunken fury. He shook me back and forth. I couldn't breathe. I was terrified. Then he suddenly flung me back on the bed with a curse. In a sober fury he might have beaten me, but he would never have killed me, and I suppose he wasn't quite drunk enough to do so now.

He came to bed a little while later, angrily, arrogantly. I didn't sleep for the rest of the night, and tried to stifle my sobs by hiding my face in the pillow. I had grown used to being bashed about by him in the daytime, but an unprovoked attack at night, with no argument building up to it, was petrifying. I felt that our love was well and truly dead, and that all he harboured towards me was continual resentment.

Another time he tried to strangle me was early one evening. And, of course, he was drunk. I'd made one single comment that annoyed him, and suddenly he came for me, slamming me back against the kitchen cupboards. I couldn't get his hands off my throat, and felt panicky, pleading wordlessly for him to stop. My knees were giving way, everything was red and hazy and there was loud buzzing in my eyes when his grip loosened. His mother had found us, and was tearing him off me, screaming blue murder. I suppose it nearly was.

I cried all evening, didn't sleep all night, but got up to find that things were better: his family had decided to step in. They saw no reason for any of them to stop drinking, but they told him off, warning him to leave me alone, and kept a closer eye on both of us. Goodness knows *they* led violent lives, and it was no new thing in our neighbourhood for wives to be beaten, but still they didn't want him injuring me. For which I was very grateful!

My family, of course, also came to my defence – that is, one of my uncles did. For I tried to keep as much of the misery of my marriage away from my parents as possible. It worked fairly well – what they *did* know about Fred shocked them so that they didn't dream there could be even more. But when my uncle caught sight of the bruises on my arms and face, he wasn't so easily put off with stories of clumsiness around the house. So he went straight to Fred and told him if he ever hit me again, he'd hit *him*.

This was some threat: he was a professional boxer and a very tough character indeed. Fred had heard the rumours of the man Uncle Al had accidently killed in a fight under a railway arch in East London, and took heed. He eased off me for a while. But he never apologised for any of it.

Thank God, there hasn't been any violence in this family for thirty years now. Becoming a Christian really did transform Fred – he'll always have a hot temper, but I soon realised I had nothing more to fear from his fists. I praise God that we still are a family – that the trust has come back.

Of course, any amount of reforming would be useless if I hadn't been able to forgive all that had gone before. And a woman can only forgive a man for breaking her heart if she has God's help. For myself, I hated him.

But I came to realise that the Fred whom I live with now is a different Fred. He has been spiritually 'born again' – and that means that where the ruling power in his life was once anger and hatred, it is now the Holy Spirit's peace and love. I don't say that Fred and the Holy Spirit have never disagreed with each other in the last thirty years, but not that dramatically. Fred wouldn't dream now of hurting me physically. Oh, he may get impatient with me at times, but he loves me and cares for me. That I know.

Nevertheless, I wouldn't be honest if I didn't mention one scene that occurred in our kitchen since we moved to Southampton.

It was one afternoon, when Fred was over-tired from too much preaching around, and out of sorts. He wandered into the kitchen and found me. I was very tired as well. All in all, it didn't take much before we were wrangling away at each other – doggedly, like you push at a loose tooth with your tongue, almost for the morbid delight in the pain. That sort of thing proves you *are* in a bad way. We should have known better.

Anyway, whatever it was we couldn't agree on (and in that mood, couldn't ignore) got way out of proportion.

And Fred went over the top.

One *smash* – and his tea-cup and saucer were in a thousand pieces. I nearly jumped out of my skin. As I cleaned it up (he'd stomped out to his garden in an uneasy silence) my feelings were hurt. But try as I could, I kept coming to the same conclusion: I was proud of my Fred.

For after three attempted stranglings in the first five years of marriage, what's a broken teacup and saucer in the following thirty years?

They weren't even expensive.

5. *When you think your marriage is over*

In the dark men break into houses ... Job 24:16

Anyone who hears Fred speak in public will gather very quickly that he has spent time in prison. And in our case, as the Bible verse promises, God really did 'set the prisoner free'.

Not all that many wives (fortunately) ever find themselves sitting in court hearing sentence passed on their husband. Even fewer then hear a sentence being passed on them as well, for something they didn't do. Both are indeed terrible experiences. Fred was sent to prison twice during our marriage, once for two years and once for five years, while I was sent away for nine months, implicated in one of his crimes. It was this, more than anything, that nearly ended our marriage. I'd had enough of Freddie Lemon and his whole lawless family.

I'd suspected Fred was a thief, of course. All the comings and goings at that house in Barking! Fred was always bringing home nice things for the house. When he first began to bring home the stolen goods, he was careful to 'explain' it to me, and I believed him. He'd say, 'Here's a bit of extra stuff I've managed to pick up.'

And there was the money! Fred had a great name in Barking for living like a king. He and his mates spent money very freely indeed – especially down at the local pub.

This thieving had gone on for several years – Fred's mother and step-father were heavily involved in it. But I didn't fully realise how serious it was until the police arrived. I'd suspected, but was frightened to say anything.

After his first spell in prison I wasn't so naive. And when he returned, it wasn't long before I began to fear that he had started up again. I lived with it because I had to – other than go to the police and betray my own husband, what could I do? I got very angry about it at times and many times tried to get him to stop stealing, but it was so hard to talk to him. We always had a roomful of people around; I was busy with my children as well, and with all the people coming and going, it was hard to figure out what was going on. When I tried to face Fred and his friends with it, and asked, 'What are you doing?' they'd laugh at me. They were all happy to steal, and they made quite a living at it. Nowadays I feel sorry for them, because that was all they knew. It sounds funny saying that an adult person is not responsible for his own actions, but that is very often the case.

And so the goods came and went – it was never a question of trying to get Fred to give them back. His temper was so violent that I just kept out of the way as much as I could, and let him get on with it. They got shot of the things they stole as soon as they could – everything from tea to tobacco to personal effects.

The first time he was caught by the police was when they found stolen goods in our house. He went to prison for two years. It came as a terrible shock to me, but is dim in my memory compared to the second time ...

It came right out of the blue one day when some policemen arrived at our house and all hell broke loose in our family. Fred had nearly killed someone! He and some mates had savagely attacked an elderly gentleman, whose house they were robbing, when he discovered them. Fred had beaten him with a lead pipe or something. The man was in a coma for seventeen days. If he had died, Fred would have hung. I don't think I fully realised the gravity of the situation at the time; all I remember was being furious with Fred, and thinking that whatever he got, he jolly well deserved. I knew he would be a long time in prison.

Then came the worst shock of all: the police came to believe that Fred's sister and I had been involved in some way as well. Nothing we could say would persuade them otherwise.

We were both put under arrest.

I remember standing in court and hearing myself sentenced to prison for the alleged involvement. No one would believe that not only were Alice and I innocent, we'd been absolutely ignorant of the whole thing. We were to serve nine months.

People have told me since that I went white to the lips. Certainly I remember that I was led away in a daze. I'll never forget that moment in court as long as I live. Having Fred in so much trouble had seemed terrible, but this was a catastrophe beyond imagining. I was innocent!

My parents were very shocked and upset, as were Fred's family. They rallied around and parcelled out the children amongst themselves.

I was taken to Holloway prison first, where it was to be decided what was to be done with me. I didn't scream or cry, I guess I must have been dazed with shock.

Then I was made to strip and have a cold bath. For an

only child, and modest by nature, I felt shamed and sick. Still stark naked, I was made to undergo a complete physical examination by one of the coldly efficient prison nurses. She treated me like a piece of meat, as she examined me for lice and venereal disease.

As I sat there, shivering with humiliation and cold, I think I hated Fred more than at any time before or since.

Something snapped inside me at that moment. I would never forgive him for this, and I would never go back to him, not ever. All his violence and drinking, and even his three attempts to kill me had not had half the effect of this examination.

I didn't *think* my marriage was over. I *knew* it was. I hated even the thought of him. I had quite a temper, and if I'd seen him at that moment, I really do believe I would have done him an injury. Fortunately, he was safe from me in Dartmoor!

'All right, Lemon, that's it. You're okay. You can get down now.' Numbly I scrambled down. They gave me prison clothes to wear – a long dark frock, dark stockings, and heavy shoes. I put them on and it dawned on me that there was something wrong with the shoes.

Then I realised what it was. One was far bigger than the other. It looked so funny, so ridiculous, so awful, that I started to giggle, and then whooped with laughter. I couldn't stop.

I did stop, though, when the warden came and slapped me hard across the face. I started to cry and cry and I couldn't stop that either. They didn't try to make me stop, though, they just led me to a cell and left me. I thought my heart would break.

Shortly after that I was taken out again and brought before the head warden of Holloway, who I remember was kind to me in her own brisk way.

'What are you doing here, Lemon?'

'I'm sure I don't know, madam,' I replied, which was indeed the truth.

'Now look, don't you be cheeky with me, I'll not stand for it.'

'I'm not being cheeky, I really don't know. I'm innocent of the crime they say I've committed.'

She looked at me sharply, and rustled through some papers. Whether I was innocent or not was not a matter she would discuss with me, but she didn't think either that I belonged in Holloway. Instead she had me sent on to Askham Grange, in Yorkshire, an open prison where inmates stayed on their honour, in comparable comfort and freedom – though woe betide you if you escaped and they caught you.

So I went to Askham Grange, along with Fred's sister. We decided quickly that of course we would stick our nine months, and felt tremendous relief and gratitude that things had not turned out worse for us.

I knew how to use a sewing machine, and so was put on the team that made men's shirts: by the time I left, I could make one and half shirts a day. We all had different jobs, and I felt sorry for the girls who worked in the garden, cleaning out the pond, etc. when the weather was so cold and bitter.

Perhaps you'll find this hard to believe, but after the initial shock of finding myself in prison at all (with the novel experience of eating my meals alongside women who'd done any number of things, including murdering their own children) I didn't find the day-to-day life too bad at all. The routine, if boring, was at least undemanding. We had all the food we could eat, and there was a certain security. Perhaps it was because I am on the whole easy-going, perhaps because I knew I was innocent, and so didn't spend hours promising myself that I'd never go wrong again. This was just nine months that I had to get through, and I decided to make the best of it.

The biggest worry of my life, Fred, had been resolved. The mental anguish that had haunted me for years had gone. I was through with Fred. I could never go back. You could almost say that I had a good rest in prison!

I worried, of course, about my children who were being taken care of by my relatives, but to be quite honest, I rarely thought of Fred. The small daily events within the prison were quite enough for me. The shirts, the meals, the other inmates, the wardens (one who tried unsuccessfully for months to get me to pronounce her very difficult surname correctly), the occasional dances in the large hall, the silly rumours that went the rounds that the hall was actually haunted by a ghostly horse and rider ... very humdrum, very unimportant, totally unconnected to the rest of my life, but I then wanted to forget the past, and the future was completely unknown, except for my one resolve. It was enough for me.

Nine months later I was released. I returned to Barking, desperately anxious to see the children again. But the house was empty and I could find none of Fred's family. Neighbours finally told me where the kids were – with my mum, with Fred's relatives. They seemed happy enough and well looked after. For years they didn't know where I had been. I wouldn't let anyone tell them. I'd just been away.

They accepted me back quite naturally. June had stayed with an aunt and little cousin her own age. She remembered me and was glad to see her mum again. It was Joyce, who stayed with Fred's mum, who'd run into problems. She was found one night in her nightgown soaking wet and wandering barefoot down the high street on her own. Some men found Joyce as they came out of a pub, and got her back home. Fred's mum didn't even know she'd been out – she was beginning to go very much her own way.

I had lain in prison and worried only about my three mites – little about Fred, other than to think how I hated him. Having got the children back I had shock number two. We had no home to live in. Well, that is not quite correct: we still had a house, but nothing inside it. Everything we'd owned had been pawned – except for two beds and a few shabby belongings. I put John down and walked around the empty rooms, seething with rage. What a state to get into. What a crazy set-up.

I stayed on at the house. There was nowhere else to go. We moved in, slept in the two beds, and began setting up house once more, trying to put a home back together on whatever I could earn.

Actually, they were very peaceful years – for his family were totally, though not cruelly, indifferent. Except for Eddie, Fred's brother, and the biggest boozer of the lot in days gone by. He took it on himself to visit me once a week, with a shilling for each of the kids, so that they could have pocket money. It was brief, no more than five minutes, but he was concerned that I was okay, and not suffering for the lack of anything. By that time my mother was dead, and my dad very ill himself. I lived quietly. It was hard to face the neighbours – to live again among the same people in the same road, my life open to all. They all knew where I had been and where Fred was. I had to live it down. They were not very friendly to start off with. The only way I lived it down was by shutting myself away. Odd jobs, and a bit of help kept us going. With four years of Fred's sentence to go, my plans were vague beyond knowing that I would stay here until he came out, and then take the children and find a home elsewhere. I didn't miss him one bit.

I was pretty shattered inside. Life was difficult enough without brooding on Fred. Though my indifference didn't stop his letters coming, letters full of anger and bitterness; nor, I'm sorry to say, equally angry letters of mine going straight back to Dartmoor. We expended a sizeable amount of paper and ink in recriminations and bitterness. Fred had actually got it into his head that I shopped him to the police and that it was my fault that he was in Dartmoor!

When a husband is responsible for sending an innocent wife to prison, and then comes to believe that the wife has sent *him* to prison – how dead can a marriage get? Stone dead, I decided. And shrugged my shoulders. That for me would have been the end anyway. I'd had it with Freddie Lemon. I just carried on taking the children back and forth to school, and discovered that if I could get a jumper knitted, the price I'd get for it would buy them a nice roast for Sunday lunch, with the proper trimmings.

And then – God stepped in. And He started with Fred. Maybe He thought it would be asking too much of my sincere but slender faith if He urged me to forgive Fred before I saw any change in him.

If you've ever read *Breakout*, or heard Fred speak, you know the story. He was in his cell one night, torn between the desire to try and escape, and interested in what a Methodist minister who visited the prison had to say, when suddenly three men appeared to him in his cell. Fred, it's Jesus, one of them said ...

And after that night, for the first time in his life, Fred realised that God was a personal God, and that He loved him, and that He had died for the sins which had landed

Fred in prison. Nothing would ever be the same again.

The process of healing, including the healing of our marriage, began.

The first I knew about it was when a very different sort of letter arrived from Fred. It was so different, in fact, from the ones I'd been getting that I sat down and read it through three times and even then could hardly believe my eyes. Was this from *my* Fred Lemon?

He said that he'd met a Methodist minister at Dartmoor, that there were meetings he'd attended, that he was becoming a Christian, and was going to give up his past life. Would I please forgive him and come back to him?

I couldn't believe my eyes! I remember I went cautiously at first. As I sat and thought about it, and prayed, I knew that I was going to give him another chance. My resolve to leave him had been based only on despair and on a determination to leave the kind of life we had led in Barking behind forever. As for Fred himself – well, if he *were* prepared to change ...

Slowly the letters between us grew fonder. I sent him pictures of myself and the children, which he happily pinned up on the wall of his cell and showed off to his fellow prisoners. 'That's my Dorothy Lamour girl,' he told them proudly. They were much too polite to contradict him, but must have had quite a chuckle over that in private, because I've always been as thin as a rail, something which the well proportioned Dorothy Lamour was *not!*

I didn't want Fred to be able to say that he had not had a chance, though I must confess, I didn't hold out much hope. It wasn't that I didn't think he *wanted* to change; what I wondered was, *could* he change!

Which made me decide one thing for sure. If this marriage was to go on, we had to live somewhere other than that house in Barking. Since my return from Askham Grange, I'd led a quiet life and had had no trouble with boozey men, but I knew that the minute Fred returned to the neighbourhood, they'd be on our doorstep in no time at all. And the pull of their way of life would prove just too strong – these were Fred's haunts, too many memories of his past life were here.

As the time for Fred's release grew nearer, I had a visit from Fred's minister friend from prison. He came full of smiles, full of joy at the change in Fred's life. He shook my hand and gave me a nice smile, but my concern made me very prim and a bit severe. After the greeting I said sternly: 'I'll give Fred one last chance. Any drinking and carousing – well, Fred can do it alone. I'm not prepared to take any more, and quite honestly, I don't think it is going to last.'

'Well, now, Mrs Lemon, I assure you ... ' He looked a bit shocked. But he hadn't had to live with Fred for years! One thing he did agree with totally – Fred and I had to leave Barking. We had to give up his family, give up my people, and clear right out of London. It was the only way. A new lifestyle and new faces for a new life.

As I prayed about it, I only knew God had done something, against all odds, in my Freddie, and that it would be wrong of me to not forgive him, and not give him another try. I suppose I still had some sort of love for him, deep down, not quite driven out. Life with Fred, even with the inevitable ups and downs, was what I still wanted.

Meanwhile, the day of Fred's release from Dartmoor was nearly upon us. Then one day the message came that Fred had been taken by the Rev. Holmes to Southampton, and that if I really was intent on having another go at our marriage, I should come on down with the children. A house had been found. Would I come or not?

This was it, then. Good-bye to Barking forever. Time to pack.

As I closed the front door and looked around us I felt a bit apprehensive. Five years is a long time. And the last time we'd seen each other was hardly under the best circumstances. He seemed to have changed so much. What would he be like, this husband of mine? Fred, a Christian. It seemed like a contradiction in terms.

6. *Back from Dartmoor*

If they obey and serve him, they will spend the rest of their days in prosperity. Job 36:11

I hired a lorry in Barking to take me and the children to Southampton. I didn't have much of a household, but we piled on what there was of it. I just hoped that those loving letters from Fred in prison would count for something once we'd got back together.

I suppose packing those things on the back of that lorry and motoring down to Southampton to resume my marriage to Fred was the biggest single positive act of forgiveness I have ever made.

Joe Blinko found us a house in Southampton – he'd motored down from Cumberland to meet Fred and had been the one to send me the message that now was the time to come. He and Fred helped us off the back of the lorry when we arrived, and we unpacked our things into a snug little cottage someone in the Methodist Hall had given us.

I felt apprehensive. I hadn't seen Fred for five years, I had never been to Southampton, and I didn't know a soul among these Christians with whom Fred was settling in. I just remember being very conscious that God had done something in Fred's life, and that I should encourage him and give him a chance to start again, if that was what he really wanted. I knew that was what *I* wanted.

It was a bit awkward at first – Fred and I had a lot of reacquainting to do. He was different already – more subdued, and a bit dazed with all that was happening. He was very grateful to be out of prison, and glad to see me and the children again. He was my Fred, and yet not the Fred I remembered.

I was a bit shy of all the Christians at the Methodist Central Hall, but every one was so kind to us – everything that anyone could have done for us was done. It was a tremendous relief to meet such friendly people!

And it was at the Central Hall that Fred and I stood together one night to make a commitment of our lives to God. Before that night I had had a reverence and a deep belief in God, but I had rarely prayed about my problems, and I didn't feel I had a personal relationship with Him. To be honest, I didn't know such a thing was possible.

God had always been in and out of my life through the years. I don't ever remember a time when He wasn't – not even as a child. Mum had taught me to pray, and I kept on praying while a child even without her continued guidance. Dad was devoutly religious, and used to take me along to a small group of Christians he regularly attended near us.

My prayers then were not as they are today, but more: 'Look after Mum, don't let anything happen to so and so ...' As I grew older I did love God and believe in Him. But my knowledge was limited. We children in Bermondsey were not taught about God in the same way as children are today at lively churches: we just accepted what we were told and were never taught to rummage around the Bible and find these things for ourselves. But I have never stopped believing in Him – indeed the horrors of the war only strengthened my faith. Seeing little children blown to bits only made me more sure that there must be a God somewhere who'd redress these terrible wrongs. It would be unbearable if that was just an end to it.

And so the night that I asked Jesus to be my personal Saviour was tremendous. I was just bursting with love and gratitude to this God whom I'd never experienced so personally before. Here He'd not only given me back this husband of mine who stood beside me, but He'd died so that I could have eternal life as well. The tears came as we knelt at the Methodist Central Hall, but they were tears of relief. I'd found God and recovered my husband. What a blessed woman I was! Who could ask for more in life?

And so we settled in Southampton. We got jobs, and started going regularly to the Central Hall. Of course some people whispered behind Fred's back: 'Oooh look, there is that jailbird that Joe picked up.' I was angry when I heard about these whisperings and felt very sympathetic towards Fred. But other Christians befriended us, and we had people in and out of the house. We still see them today, and they are wonderful friends.

Fred's new ways came gradually, as you'd expect. He must have worried about his people back in Barking, but he never said that he wanted to go back to them. We used to sit up sometimes at night after the children were asleep, and talk about the house we had been given, Fred's job prospects and the new arrangements, and wonder how it would all turn out in the end. Would our 'second' marriage succeed?

Well, we are both still here more than thirty years later, and Fred is still going around telling people what

God has done in his life. I believe that his faith means everything in the world to him.

As for me, I don't preach, and I don't testify in public, but I too have learned a lot through our experience. Fred's conviction and mine turned out to be the crisis point in our marriage. I thank God that He brought such long-term good out of it. Dartmoor was both the worst thing and the best thing that ever happened to us.

I wonder sometimes what would have happened if we'd been left to carry on in Barking, to tear each other slowly apart with our arguments. I don't honestly see how our marriage would have survived. I would have taken the children and left. I wouldn't have brought them up through their adolescence in an atmosphere like that.

I wouldn't of course recommend a spell in prison for every couple that isn't getting on, but in our case it certainly did wonders! Our enforced separation gave us both time to be alone, for God to work in both our hearts and for Him to begin to draw us together again, as different, whole people.

It would have been hard in those early months if we'd had to live with each other as well: too much opportunity for us to shout at each other and not let the Holy Spirit get a word in edgeways! You could almost say that in the far-reaching plans of God, Fred's years in prison were used in the way you see squabbling children separated and put alone until they calm down.

Obviously, God did not send Fred to prison, but His power for good is so great, that if we let Him, He can bring good out of the greatest human tragedy. It is a wicked world, and as God has given people true free will and the power to carry out their desires, there is much evil. But He is always hovering by, and will gladly redeem us and begin to salvage our lives.

Fred and I learned a lot about what to do when you think your marriage is over and, more importantly, how it can be saved. We learned that when a marriage is on the rocks, the one place where you begin is *not* in straightening out the marriage but in straightening out the people involved.

In our case, God started in sorting out Fred. Maybe that was the easier task! I had a lot of anger and bitterness and even hatred, so perhaps God knew I would only be reached if I knew the Almighty had dealt with my husband first!

God is the most important thing in life, far more important than even your marriage. You can't use God as a marriage broker, who will come in and change your mate, put your marriage back together, and pat you both on the head and leave you to lead your own lives.

Your spiritual standing before God comes first. If your marriage is over, let it drift a while, while you get right with God. Because He cares about you, He cares about your marriage. Leave it to Him.

When you let the Holy Spirit convict you of wrong-doing, and turn from your sins, you begin to change. You begin to see where you have been wrong in your ways with other people, and you begin (it can be a long process) to sort yourself out. Not with the underlying motive of saving a marriage, but because that is your responsibility to God.

I don't believe it is really until then that a person is spiritually, and hence emotionally and mentally, equipped to deal with a difficult marriage. Because it isn't going to be easy to get a dismal relationship off the rocks. There is a heap of forgiving and forgetting to do if things can ever be repaired between you.

But even getting right with God yourself isn't a

guarantee that your marriage problems are over. Please don't expect a simple success formula for 'How to save your marriage in three simple steps'. It is just not true.

God *will* work in people's lives through His Holy Spirit if you pray for them. But He woos, He does not force. People with difficult spouses should pray for them, but remember that that spouse is still free to say no. When you pray for your spouse, how petty to say: 'Dear God, my husband is a rotter. Please show him how awful he is and please make him far nicer to live with. Amen.'

I don't think such a prayer will be answered. The world does not revolve around me or you. It revolves around Christ, and it is to Him that people owe their allegiance. He is their creator. So start praying for your husband not that he will be better, but that he will turn to God and find Him.

And if your husband does begin to find God, then you both may have a long way to go, but you are at least beginning with the surest foundation that there is.

If you think your marriage is over, it may be over. I can offer no tips on how to save anything and everything. I can't say to you: 'Look, you think you've got problems; I've had them worse than that. So don't worry – if I came through, so can you.'

Not necessarily so.

For it is not the outward things that really matter in the end. You may have been far more civilised and discreet than Fred and I and still break up. It's not how far down you go (though if it is any comfort to you, I don't think it's possible to get lower than Fred and I were) but how you respond to God. It cannot be done in your own strength. If it gives you comfort to think, 'My, Fred and Doris went through all that and still came out'

– well and good, but remember that we could have gone through a lot less and still separated if we had not turned to Christ.

Which brings me to the other important lesson I've learned. St. Paul was realistic and accepted that even Christian marriages might end. He never said: 'If you're a good Christian and pray, hey presto, you'll have a great marriage'. He recognised people have free choices in responding to God – including awkward partners!

But *both* of you have to respond – and in our case, that meant me as well! For of course all our rowing was not entirely Fred. It takes two to break a marriage. I decided I wanted things to go my way. I brooded over our unhappiness a lot, and shed quite a few tears. I'm sure that some of those awful days were my fault. I don't completely blame Fred. I expect I was just as hard for him to live with, in my own way. How different I was from his sisters! They were carefree and casual, but I was more proper. I wouldn't drink, and wouldn't hold wild parties, and that must have irritated him no end. Looking back, I sometimes wonder if a lot of our arguments and rows may have been due to misunderstanding.

When Fred came out of Dartmoor, how easy it would have been for me to be vindictive and self-righteous, and refuse to forgive. I had excellent reasons for doing so – years of bitter experience! To forgive all that requires mercy, a desire to give him yet another chance, though he had used up many chances before.

When both of us responded to the prompting of the Holy Spirit, and determined to live close to God, and close to one another, God's lavish goodness and help astounded me. It came in the form of those Christians in Southampton thirty years ago. How kind they were!

What could have been an excruciatingly difficult, poverty-stricken time for our family was smoothed over. We were given a flat and furniture – then a cottage, and later a three-bedroomed house. Truly what Paul called the body of Christ, was working to care for us. It gave Fred and me a chance to start again, without unbearable material hardships and worries.

I am eternally thankful to those Christians. God used them to help in our tentative efforts to rebuild our marriage. I felt a bit overwhelmed at times by all the kindness shown to us. So if you want to serve God, and don't think you are the marriage guidance counsellor type, or an evangelist or pastor, don't worry. The little gift of hospitality that Paul mentions in the Bible is one of the biggest as far as I'm concerned. Fred and I knew practical love, practical help. That it was the Church should be doing – giving people a chance to start again. After the initial counselling and preaching, what we really needed was a roof over our head every night, clothes for the children, job help for Fred ...

So don't envy the big, public gifts. Hospitality and care among Christians is so desperately needed. God used those humble generous Christians to save our marriage just as much as any minister, by keeping us out of the dangerous (for us) area of East London.

When Fred became a Christian, I felt he began to love me again. His attitude towards me changed very much as the months went by. I was mostly home with all the children, but I noticed it very much – and it really meant something. If we'd travelled his preaching circuit and he'd been nice to me, it wouldn't have counted half as much as his increasing thoughtfulness and kindliness and generosity in the privacy of his own home, with no audience.

I'm so glad I came back to him. He's become a real

homelover, and since Dartmoor, has always been glad to come home to me. We like to sit with our feet up, watching the football and drinking tea.

7. Does he bite your head off?

Starting a quarrel is like breaching a dam; so drop the matter before a dispute breaks out. Proverbs 17:14

I come home one afternoon from shopping in Southampton to be greeted by Fred looking rather upset. He waves a shirt at me.

'Do you call this ironed?' he says. 'I can't wear this to the meeting tonight. Wrinkles everywhere ...' He clutches it tightly in his large hands and holds it out for inspection, but the only wrinkles I can see are those of his making.

I make my way past him down the hall and sigh to myself. Here we go. I put down my packages, aware that Fred is still talking.

'... tell you time and again how to do it. Can't you even iron a shirt?'

I turn and face him. 'I'm sorry,' I say simply, and mean it.

He continues as if I hadn't spoken. 'Where is this iron? I'll do it myself. But it's going to make me late. You know how I like my shirts ...'

I take off my coat and calmly hang it up. I pick up my groceries and quietly head for the kitchen. Fred follows at my heels.

'You don't get the iron hot enough.'

I put my groceries down on the table and turn away from Fred to go to the kettle. He follows me to the stove. 'You don't steam them enough.' He follows me to the sink as I fill the kettle. 'A shirt needs steam.' He backs up a step as I turn and walk calmly back to the stove. 'You know how I like my shirts.'

The cat wants to come in. I go to the kitchen door, through our side porch, and out to the back door. Fred follows, six inches behind me. 'You're no use at all ironing my shirts if you don't do them properly the first time.'

I open the door and the cat comes in. There is a slight bottleneck as the cat greets me and the three of us – and the shirt – get turned around and head, single file, back to the kitchen.

'I can't wear this tonight.'

'It looks okay to me,' I suggest softly. But it's a mistake. While the water heats Fred goes off into a detailed discussion, pointing out why the shirt is, in fact, *not* okay. I miss most of it because I am feeding the cat and don't bother to look up. Fred does not notice this, as he is peering at the shirt from a distance of about six inches, holding it up to the light.

The water boils and I make tea.

'You can't expect me to preach in a shirt that looks like I've slept in it,' Fred concludes bitterly.

It is difficult to avoid looking at or bumping into someone as large as Fred in our small kitchen, but I'm an expert with years of experience. I pick up my mug, and wander off down the hall into the living room.

'Tea's there, love,' I call back. 'Don't let it get cold.'

I'm enjoying a rest, watching the news with my feet up, when he comes in a few minutes later, nearly ready to go. He is wearing another shirt which I have ironed for him. He sits down at the table and we finish our tea together. I look up and catch his eye briefly, reading the signs. Yes, it's played out.

'Never mind, love,' he says peaceably.

A few minutes later it's time for him to leave. I walk with him to the car. Fred takes me into his arms, and gives me a great hug. I stand on tiptoe and raise my face to be kissed.

'Take care now. I won't be home late.'

'All right,' I say. 'Drive carefully. Hope it goes well.'

He climbs into the car, we smile cheerfully at each other, he waves his hand, and drives off. I wish him well, and pray that God will bless his speaking as I return to the homely company of an evening's television. The cat is still in the kitchen as I fill the kettle for another cup of tea. With just the two of us the room seems very quiet and empty. I smile to myself and agree with the poet who once wrote: 'Peace, perfect peace, with loved ones far away!'

And that is how Freddie and I live with his temper these days. It's just like one of those storms on the Sea of Galilee in Israel – it can blow up anytime, anywhere, for any reason and can range fiercely. But then, just as suddenly, it's gone, and everything is fine once more.

And I really mean 'fine'. That is one of the things I love about Fred – he never holds a grudge, never makes recriminations, never sulks. When he is angry with me, he wants to tell me all about it, but then that's that. Two minutes later it is all forgotten. Provided, of course, I don't hit back, or try to defend myself. Once upon a time I did – in the days when such things mattered to me. And of course, in those days Freddie's temper had to be seen to be believed!

For never mind Fred's wild drinking, or his violence: we could have torn our marriage apart with just our tongues. In fact, of all the problems in our marriage, Fred's caustic, biting tongue has always hurt me the most. I couldn't have survived if I hadn't come to terms with it. And it doesn't take long for criticism and sharpness to destroy a love, – but then any woman with a critical husband will tell you that.

I first felt the edge of Fred's tongue soon after I married him. It came as quite a shock. Of course, I wasn't the first to encounter it; Fred's temper had got him into trouble for years. He would lash out at every and anyone. But being in love with him made me peculiarly vulnerable. He used to criticise me for every little thing, and would sometimes deliberately set out to humiliate and belittle me in front of other people.

Learning to cope with it took me years. I spent a lot of time fighting back at first. I don't know now where I got the courage from, but I wasn't going to be walked over; I was determined to stand up for myself. So I'd end by getting a clout, or he'd reach for my throat.

I spent a lot of time in tears. I recall one evening we had a particularly nasty go at each other, with me sobbing the whole time. Fred, on the other hand, after a few last vitriolic comments, sauntered off down the pub for a pint with his mates, leaving me alone in the house in the dimming twilight, weeping my heart out. After I calmed down, I got to thinking long and hard. It was always me who was crying, never him. He had no regrets. So why on earth should I? It was the beginning of a resolve never to cry in front of him again.

I'm afraid my new resolve was also matched by a growing indifference. A woman's love can take only so many knocks. I became harder towards him, just to survive. In fact, in the end, I couldn't have cared less what he said or thought. I began to go my own sweet way.

That's of course, when woman often start to look around for someone else who will be kind and loving to them. But I never once looked for another man. I didn't want anybody else; I just wanted Fred to behave himself.

My new tactics were quite simple: I simply decided one day that I would no longer argue back. With violent and quarrelsome husbands, it's really the best thing to do. If a man's in a foul temper already, you'll achieve nothing by rubbing him up the wrong way. When he was angry, I learned to keep my mouth shut no matter how he moaned and found fault. It worked. Whatever someone says, if you don't answer, they can't keep on going indefinitely. They are talking to themselves. So when words began between us, I'd just go upstairs to turn out the bedrooms and let him work in the garden. If he was really angry, I'd walk the streets for hours, looking in shop windows. Though I would give myself the satisfaction of slamming the door as I left the house!

Of course, all this suggests total indifference to his anger and impatience. And this is where God comes in. For over the years I have prayed a lot about our arguments. God has given me the grace to get by, and after I pray, I feel calmed, and can recover a proper perspective. God helps me to forgive him and to love him. Fred can't help being what he is. I blame a lot on his past life, and make all the allowances that I can.

If it hadn't been for my faith in God, I don't know what I would have done. Knowing that I always have Somebody who loves me, I don't need Fred's approval.

Mind you, Fred doesn't erupt anymore, he just percolates. God really has worked miracles in him. We have tiffs, but they blow over. If he bites my head off, I know he'll be sweet a minute later. And whatever may have happened between us during the day, when bedtime comes, we forget it. We say goodnight peaceably and start afresh the next day. Even if we have a grumble just before he leaves on a weekend's preaching engagement, he'll ring me as he always does when he's away, and by then any hard words or feelings will have been well and truly forgotten.

If you've a critical husband, don't let him destroy you. Women are so vulnerable to their men; but don't base your sense of self-worth on a man's valuation of you. Remember, God loves you and accepts you. Keep calm, keep your sense of perspective. God wants us to live in peace and He's right – life is much too short to be always upset and arguing.

The next time Fred gets irritable, I'm going to clean out our wardrobe. It needs it anyway – I'm just waiting for an argument that's worth taking the two hours needed to do it!

8. *It's the thought that counts*

The wise woman builds her house, but with her own hands the foolish one tears hers down   Proverbs 14:1

It is a fine, sunny summer afternoon in Southampton, and I am standing at my kitchen sink. Suddenly the door swings wide and Fred's tall, broad frame fills the doorway. He flings a book onto the kitchen table. Without even looking my way, he turns abruptly on his heel, and says gruffly: 'That's for you.'

The door shuts behind him.

I have just been given a present.

'Thank you very much!' I call after him, though expecting (and getting) no reply. I smile to myself as I examine what he's brought me. Whatever happened to those loving, attentive men you see on the telly who risk fire and death and avalanche to present a woman with a box of chocolates? Or, as in the romances, men who take women in their arms and say huskily: 'Here darling, these diamonds are for you because I love you madly?'

It's a good book. With my tea towel I brush a few crumbs off the surface and put it on the chair to go upstairs. I look forward to reading it and appreciate Fred's kind thought.

For that's what it was.

And though I'm not in the business of handing out advice, if there is one thing I would plead with women to do, it is to *understand* your man. I could fill a book just on that subject (I suppose that's because it has taken me so many years to understand Fred, that I'm proud of having at last mastered my subject!)

And the key thing in understanding anyone is to look behind their actions and try and discover their motives. Men can sometimes seem to women like those friendly foreign tourists who pour into Britain each summer. Most of their actions are fine and understandable, but every so often they do something which seems very strange and irritates you. Assuming they *are* friendly and mean well, it's worth remembering that their actions result from a totally different outlook on life, and therefore aren't necessarily meant in the way in which they can come across to *you*. Americans, for instance, wear dazzlingly bright clothes not in order to blind the English, but because they think it makes them attractive!

Apply this principle to a man, and hey presto – you might discover that he's far nicer than you ever thought! Or at least he *intends* to be – and does all he can to be so.

For instance, consider the frying pan in my kitchen. No ordinary model this, but a great super de luxe beast that stands haughtily on its four elegant legs, taking up all the space on my only free table. It is electric, operated by dials and switches that it took my son three weeks to persuade me to touch. It does roasts, custards, cakes, everything – enough for a hungry family of six. And – you guessed it – it's a present from Fred. To be used for just the two of us.

We'd been slowly wandering through one of those huge kitchenware departments at a store in

Southampton one afternoon and when we got back to the car Fred had this huge box in brown paper in his hands (yes, he *had* paid for it!). He opened the back door of the car and dumped it on the rear seat.

'Here,' he said. 'You should use that.'

I was mystified, and spent the return journey half in the front seat and half in the back, tearing at the paper in some trepidation, wondering what I'd been landed with this time. The price was left on: £40 it read. That really startled me.

'Fred, what on earth *is* it?'

'It's the thing nowadays,' he said airily. 'Housewives use 'em. Far better for cooking.'

'Oh?' I said warily, totally unconvinced that Fred knew the first thing about what housewives really used. In sheer disbelief I finally drew out this huge, vast *basin* of a frying pan.

'Nice and roomy,' he commented. True. It took up half the seat.

'Yes,' I replied carefully, refraining from adding: 'I could feed half the street out of this thing!' The on/off, hot/simmer controls looked so much like 'high technology' to me that I wouldn't have been surprised if it had turned into a small UFO and sailed away.

'Fred, thank you,' I said heartily as we pulled up outside our house. 'This is super. It's smashing. Er – could you carry it in for me?'

He smiled nonchalantly. ''Course. Now get the door open and move out of the way.' He staggered into the house with it. I smiled up at his broad back and thought, 'Freddie Lemon, you're daft, but I love you!'

Only one slight tiff over that one. Fred wanted his dinner in it that night, but I refused to touch it without some advice. 'Suppose it blows up, or something?' He looked on and muttered scornfully as my small, reliable old frying pan was placed on the stove. So dinner was somewhat strained (but it *was* done to perfection!)

The key to living peaceably with Freddie is to remember that his heart sometimes springs into action without proper directions from his head. For in these past few years he has become very generous, and since our retirement he has quietly got on with jobs to improve our home.

But no matter that the loo door has seized up on its hinges and closing it for the past few weeks requires me to fling myself on it in fury, bracing my feet somewhere between the sink and the loo; or that Freddie's bookcase in the living room is groaning with stacks of books and papers in emminent danger of toppling off. When Fred donated a spare day to home improvement, he took it into his head to repaper and paint our bedroom. He went and chose both paper and paint himself, and stoutly got underway as soon as I left for shopping and a visit to my daughter.

Our bedroom didn't *need* the work, and so I was stunned when he led me upstairs to show it to me that evening.

'Ooh Fred – it's beautiful!' I exclaimed. 'It's really smashing!'

For why hound a man for the things he hasn't done when you can encourage the things that he has? I was delighted that he'd taken the trouble, picked colours I liked, and had wanted to surprise me. And, I admit it, I was very pleased to discover he'd done such an excellent job! He leaned comfortably against the door frame and scratched his cheek.

'Not bad, eh Doris?'

We were both very proud of him.

No matter what your husband does, before you lay into him with moans, complaints, or appeals to reason, do stop and try to see things from his point of view. Don't just consider the outward things. Look at the outward things in relation to the man himself. A cup of tea from one man can be as much an achievement as a four course meal and a trip to the theatre from another.

Consider his background: if his mother has waited on him hand and foot all his life, don't be surprised when he doesn't race you to do the washing up. He's not being chauvinistic – he's simply coping with womenfolk in the way he's been taught. Freddie's had no background of loving care whatsoever, and so his generosity is a bit hit-and-miss at times. But he's learning.

Consider his temperament. Some men are affable all the time on the surface, but still selfish and possessive underneath. Fred can be moody at times, but he gives me all I need, and lets me go out and about Southampton as I please. It might never occur to him to come waltzing into the kitchen humming a love song, present me with a box of chocolates and cover me with kisses, crooning 'I love you madly' (if he did, I'd die of shock) but that doesn't mean he doesn't love me, and think about me. He's more simple, straightforward, undemonstrative. But if I took that to mean indifference or callousness on his part, how tragically wrong I'd be.

If you moan when your husband's generosity seems a little eccentric, you won't ensure that it's more practical next time. In all likelihood there won't be a next time!

You may think I'm saying that men can behave towards you however they like and you've just to accept it meekly and be grovellingly grateful for anything good. Nothing of the sort. Fred and I quarrelled for years over his behaviour to me. And I believe that I was right to speak up for myself, and I'd do it again. I have never let Fred walk all over me and I never will.

But if you know your husband means well, don't be too hard to please. I'm a great one for accepting any gesture of goodwill in the spirit that Fred means it; even if I can't always fathom what made him choose to do that particular thing. Like the time he took to painting doors around the house. He painted several, but only on one side. This puzzled me, but I concluded it was better to have even one side done than none at all!

For after I stood up for myself on the 'basics' (and they'll vary from woman to woman), I knew I had to be prepared to give a lot, and be tolerant. Don't let your feelings get hurt or irritated too easily. Women are prone to harbouring 'ideal' versions of their husbands in their minds, and can be often – and shrilly – disappointed with him if he doesn't live up to it. I've come to believe that every one has a right to their own personality. It's his home as much as yours, and he doesn't exist *just* to please you.

One last word on that frying pan: having mastered the controls with my son John's help, I determined to give in to Fred's request and do him a proper meal in it. I bought a roast, cautiously put it in the pan and cooked it slowly all day, with all the trimmings, according to instructions. I served it up that night as a special surprise.

Fred was in the living room watching the sport on TV. He took a few mouthfuls and stopped. 'Don't think much of your dinner tonight, Doris,' he said reproachfully. 'Your roasts are usually much better than this.'

'But that's out of your frying pan!' I cried.

'Oh.' Fred paused, gave me a quick glance, tried another forkful and then pushed back his plate. 'Ah well. Tastes funny, doesn't it?'

So that was that. From then on it's been unspokenly 'understood' between us that I'm to go back to my small frying pan on the stove. The super de luxe model has not been used in months, and by tacit agreement we both pretend it just isn't on the table anymore. Thank goodness!

9. *Why I would never divorce my husband*

What a man desires is unfailing love ... Proverbs 19:22

It is evening, quite late, and the meeting has just broken up. Over the tops of people's heads I catch a glimpse of Fred's tall broad frame, his head looking lonely and a bit bare without its semi-permanent fixture: his cloth cap.

He is surrounded by people. It seems as if everyone in the hall wants to meet him – the guest speaker who's just given a stirring testimony of God's work in his life. Some no doubt will want him to help them with their problems as well.

I sit quietly by, my handbag on both knees, preoccupied by the sad self-knowledge that I am cursed with shyness and find it hard to chat so easily with strangers. 'How does he cope with it all?' I ask myself. I like people but find so many at one time overwhelming.

Suddenly, out of the general melee of people I hear the friendly loud voice of the hostess who is kindly going to put us up for the night. 'Here she is. You really must meet her ... Doris, I must introduce you to a good friend of mine ... '

A large woman bustles up and attaches herself to my

hand, her soft white fleshy fingers squeezing tight. She is at least the twentieth stranger to greet me tonight, and I feel giddy as I try to think of something to say beyond a timid 'hello'.

'I don't know why you are here,' she booms. '*I* would certainly never put up with it. It's far too much to ask of any woman.'

I stop in amazement. Beneath her formidable exterior, at last, someone who can sympathise with shyness?

'If he was my husband, he would certainly be alone,' she continues loudly.

'Oh well, he appreciates it that I'm here,' I reply.

But what have I said? She looks at me in astonishment. 'I should say he does ... '

We both stop in confusion. 'You *do* mean tonight?' I venture.

'Tonight? Of course not! I mean at all! Why did you never divorce him?'

What an impossible question to answer right off the cuff! That's the problem of having a husband with a well-known story: strangers ask you the most intimate questions that they would never dream of asking anyone else they'd just met. They feel, of course, as if they know you because they know the story. But if Fred's testimony helps them, it is fine with me, and I don't mind such questions at all – I got used to them years ago.

'Well, I don't believe in divorce,' I begin.

'Don't believe in it? Why ever not? *I'd* have said good riddance!'

'I would have felt that to be wrong,' I explain. 'For me, anyway.'

'Wrong? He was in the wrong. I would have divorced him the first time he hit me. Mind you, it turned out okay in the end ... '

'If I had divorced him,' I said, 'I feel that it would have put me in the wrong then as well.'

I'm not getting through. She looks baffled, but grins. 'Nonsense,' she says, and taps the side of her head, good-naturedly suggesting a slight mental deficiency on my part on this point. I grin back: she's not the first who's wondered why on earth Fred and I never got divorced.

I think it all stems from the way in which I approached my marriage so many years ago now. Although I did not know God very well in a personal way, the Christian guidelines by which my parents had brought me up had affected me deeply. I felt that in taking my marriage vows I was making God a promise as much as Fred.

In our case, that was just as well, because only God and I have any recall of those vows! Poor Freddie was so drunk at the time that I'm grateful that he was able to stand up and say anything at all. He can't begin to remember those most important words that we have ever said to one another.

But no matter; we had said them. I knew from my upbringing that God intended marriage as a life long contract, and that's how it was going to be with me.

And what of the problems that came later? The drinking and violence, not to mention the thieving? Even though they gradually destroyed the relationship between us, I never thought of divorcing him. However hard I found life married to Fred, I wasn't prepared to get hurt more by going against my conscience. After all, it was 'for better, for *worse* ... '

I admit that separation looked highly attractive a number of times, not only for my sake, but for the children's sakes as they grew older. It seemed to me – and it still does – that if you just can't take the problems in a marriage any more you are at liberty to live separately. There was a time when I was burning all his letters and sending none in return. But separation is as far as I would have gone. I just wanted a straighforward life of peace in which to raise my children.

There has always been one big factor in favour of our marriage continuing, and it was one of the reasons I decided to carry on after Dartmoor: Fred never carried on with any other women. He has never been unfaithful to me. In those early years he might have been away half the night without being willing to tell me where he was, but there were only three things he was likely to be doing: robbing someone's house (though I didn't know this at the time!), getting drunk, or bashing himself up in a fight. And though any of these were hardly desirable, I would have liked it even less if he'd been carrying on with someone else.

But I never had reason to doubt him once. He was a man's man, and (except for when he fell in love with me) had never given the gentler sex much thought. I knew he was like that before we were married, and it was in fact one of the things that had first attracted me to him. Not because I fancied men with scant time for romance! But I sensed that he was making an effort to get to know me because he was really attracted to me as a person. I was not just another 'piece of skirt' to him.

I discovered it the first time he ever took me home. We had been invited to tea with his mother, and she left us alone in her front room for a while while she got ready. He made no passes at me at all, which I had slightly dreaded, but instead we chatted in a friendly way about our childhoods, London, the war ...

He was like that all during our courtship – never one for a fumble, which I would have hated. Not that he wasn't affectionate, but he rarely showed it. He found it hard to express himself that way because he'd never been shown much cuddling himself.

That fidelity of his has been very important to me. I can well see why women divorce without it: marriage becomes a farce. I definitely would have left him if he'd been unfaithful. But divorce? I don't think so, not even then. I think I would have reasoned that if he wanted to carry on with others, that was his choice. I wasn't going to live with him if he did, but neither would I divorce him. He might have lived with another woman, but he'd have remained my husband. For me, once married, always married.

Perhaps it is because I have always been pretty self-sufficient. I was an only child and though sometimes lonely, I did learn to enjoy my own company. I loved Fred and of course wanted a happy married relationship. But to be loved by a man was never an urgent priority for me at all. Had our marriage ended, I would have been through with men; I sought joy and fulfillment in my children. No divorce would be needed; I wanted no freedom to start again. Separation would have accomplished all I sought – just to have a decent life.

Of course for women who crave to be loved by a man, it must be very difficult if their marriage does not work out, and they are tempted to find comfort elsewhere. Such an idea never occurred to me. I have never wanted any man but Fred, and even when he was at his worst, I know now that deep down inside somehow I still loved him.

And what about Fred? Did he ever consider divorcing me? Well, if he did, he's never mentioned it once in our entire forty-three years of marriage! Mind you, that doesn't mean he didn't get some odd notions of jealousy in his head in those early years ...

Like the time I went swimming with our children one afternoon, to the local swimming baths. When I got back, my hair was not quite dry at the tips. I didn't say where I'd been, and without meaning to, I left a mighty puzzled and even slightly alarmed husband in the sitting room as I sailed through into the kitchen. He followed me with a funny look on his face. I hadn't been with another man, had I ...?

I think my astonishment was only matched by his rather embarrassed relief. No, of course he hadn't really thought I'd do such a thing ... No, of course, he hadn't thought of the children, the swimming baths ... he even apologised ... it was just that I hadn't mentioned it ... Thinking it over later, I came to the conclusion that he must sometimes forget that I was not like many of the other women in Barking. For of course, many unhappily married women *do* seek love elsewhere. But I'm sure, from many of the personal problems I've heard about in the past ten years through Fred's pastoral work, that a woman should stay with her husband.

I really do know what it's like not to feel loved, and to be afraid that things will never change. But I still believe that a woman should persevere with her husband, and take her vows really seriously.

If you ever contemplate divorce, do sit down and think out the true implications. There is no such thing as a really fresh start. People cannot walk away from a marriage and pretend that it never happened. There will be heartbreak, recrimination, and if there are children, lifelong effects on them too.

Turn to God. He cares about you and your marriage. He will give you wisdom and strength. He wants you to stay married.

Finally, I believe that each partner in a marriage is responsible for their behaviour first to God, not to each other. So the fact that your husband may not be a proper husband does not give you the right not to be what you should be to him.

If I had gone off with another man because Fred neglected me, it would still have destroyed him had he found out, even if he'd acknowledged that he'd brought it on himself. For all our rows, even his violence, he was always fiercely protective of me as *his* wife.

I didn't mind, but it did get a bit ridiculous at times! I shall never forget one summer evening in the early years of our marriage. It was in the days when I was young, with a good figure, and sometimes men would look twice.

I was tending our small fish stall on a corner in Barking while Fred and his 'step-father' and the rest of the family were in the local boozer. I didn't mind standing there alone on the corner at all, for one of the houses across the street had recently been the scene of some local notoriety – a murder or something had taken place there, and the road had swarmed with police and newspapermen. It was pretty quiet and dull that particular warm evening, but I kept half an eye on it anyway, just in case anything more dramatic should occur – I'm afraid I didn't want to miss it!

After a while Fred came and joined me to see how I was doing, and together we stood and watched the world go by. It was at this point an unfortunate local resident, a quiet, thin man whom Fred for some reason had never liked, made his way down the street towards us.

I'd bent down to get some more cockles as he came even with my stall. My movement caught his attention, and he glanced my way. Our eyes happened to meet.

'Evening,' he said. People spoke to each other in those days, even in London.

'Evening,' I replied politely, straightening up as he

continued on by, swinging his arms in his funny walk.

And then Fred went berserk. Suddenly, without any warning whatever, he sprang forward, slamming his great ham of a fist into the man's face. The man soared up – and down – straight into the gutter – out cold. Some coins flew out of his hand and struck me in the face – and bits and pieces from his shabby pockets scattered along the edge of the pavement and down into the road.

I was flabbergasted. Some passers-by helped bring the poor man around, and helped him move on, away from the glowering baleful eye of Fred. But Fred and I never spoke about it afterwards. I suppose Fred figured he'd been eloquent enough; I was too non-plussed and amazed to think of any comment but obvious ones – which were probably best left unsaid!

That was a very long time ago, and Fred no longer attacks people who say 'hello' to me – a comforting thing to know if you ever attend a meeting where Fred is speaking and you want to come over afterwards and introduce yourself to me!

At the meeting where we started this chapter it was quite late before Fred could get away, but our hostess kindly waited until he was finished before driving us back to her home. Fred and I sat in the back seat, and I snuggled up to him, partly to get warm and partly because of the conversation I'd had with the lady over divorce.

How glad I was that I hadn't divorced him years ago! I slid my hand into his and he smiled wearily. I pondered his face in the light of the traffic lights as the dark roads of the town flashed by.

If we had divorced, where would be both be right now? I'd have lived a lonely, comfortless existence, struggling to raise three children, with few friends on account of my shyness. My children would have had no father.

And as for Fred? He would have grown to a lonely old age (if he hadn't been hanged first) without having anyone who really cared a jot for him. It's one thing to part in anger when you are young, but loneliness when you are old is a terrible thing.

God saw us through our bad years. I believe with His help families can stick together. For better, for worse.

10. *People coming and going*

Do not forget to entertain strangers, for by so doing some people have entertained angels without knowing it. Hebrews 13:2

Fred's rough, wild 'mates' and his attachment to them was an early problem in our marriage, but the basic thing that caused it still exists: Fred's a people lover.

Fred just loves company. He's at his best with lots and lots of people around – the more, the louder, and the merrier, the better.

This household somehow has always attracted people – friends, and acquaintances Fred was trying to help, even strangers.

It hasn't been quite so hectic in recent years – now we are into our middle sixties we are both slowing down a bit and like our cup of tea in some peace and quiet. But until now – well! From the earliest days of my marriage it was clear to me that the old adage 'you marry the family as well as the man' didn't go far enough where Fred was concerned: apparently I'd married into half of Barking!

Wherever Fred went, his mates followed. He is a natural leader, and they flocked to him, and followed his example, from drinking to thieving.

And when we moved to Southampton and set up house again, it wasn't long before Fred was inviting people home, especially those in need. Fred's new faith attracted people. Many used to come time and time again, and would go to church with us on a Sunday morning. There were down-and-outs, and even men who'd just left prison. And the first thing that always seemed to occur to him was to invite them home (even murderers). Fred would talk to them while I laundered their clothes. If they thought it best that they stayed on for a few days, then I would try to make room for them. I still went out to work at this time, but I made sure that any 'guests' were out all day as well, looking for a job. Then I'd make sure that I got home first, and by the time they returned, I had the table set and the meal nearly done. I didn't mind the extra work – I wanted to do it. Our minister greatly encouraged me when he commented that he thought God was guiding me to do this.

I guess, in all, I had at least sixty men pass through this house while the children (not only my own but also the five other nephews and nieces that we adopted) were growing up. I *was* a bit worried at first that the men would bother the children, but I prayed and went ahead. God answered my prayer; the men never were anything but gentle with the children. Sometimes when they were downtown in Southampton they would get drunk and get into the most fearful brawls, but when they came home to us they behaved themselves perfectly. The couple of times one of them got a bit rude, I took off a shoe and headed straight for him – and he fled!

I would encourage women to open their homes and make themselves available to people in need. Why ever not? They are people too, and maybe they've had no chance in life. Certainly anything we gave was more than returned in some of the rich friendships that came out of our helping people – and sometimes with the most unlikely ones imaginable. I recall especially the man we nicknamed Big Geoffrey – for reasons which would be obvious if you'd seen him.

Usually when he came by we'd feed him, and tell him as kindly as we could to go upstairs and take a bath, or to go and get a haircut – or both! He responded by coming faithfully to church with us for a long time. In fact, he became so attached to the Lemon family that he wouldn't go to church without us, and would fidget around the house on a Sunday morning and swear away if we kept him waiting as we got ready for church. But he was a handful! And sometimes, I confess, when he came for a visit and I was alone I just couldn't face him. I took to hiding in a small cupboard under the stairs for a few minutes if I heard him come in the back door and call out for us. He'd have a quick look around the house, but if he thought we were all out, he'd leave. That worked well a couple of times until the day he opened the cupboard for some reason and found me crouched in there silently, peering up at him as the door swung wide. We both gave a colossal jump and had to have a cup of tea to restore our nerves. He said little about my being inside a closed cupboard in my house in the middle of the afternoon, and afterwards as I laughed over it with June, we both wondered what he'd made of it all.

Of course many of the men Fred brought home had done terrible things, and really were quite dangerous if you didn't know what you were doing. They weren't plotting against us, but they were extremely unstable people with very immature emotions and you just couldn't depend on them. You had to treat them carefully, like an unpredictable child.

I soon realised that I had to be tactful. I cared for each man: cleaned him up, and fed him in between his chat with Fred about the problems he had. Each one was so different. Some needed all the kindness you could lavish on them; others were very stubborn and forthright and you had to be quite firm with them. One of the elders at the chapel, who helped Fred from time to time with the men, told us that he had noticed that I had a 'gift of discernment' – at least that is what he called it. I don't know whether I had it or not, but from that time on my 'discerning faculties' were in great demand, and he and Fred used to send for me when they came up against a problem in one of the men that they didn't know what to do with. Did I think this, or did I think that, they would demand, and wait eagerly for my hesitant reply. I got to a stage where I could read a man's character pretty quickly. Perhaps it is because women are more intuitive than men, but I could sense a lot just from looking the man in question full in the face, and studying his eyes as I chatted with him. I'd pray as I talked, and then I'd pass on what I felt to Fred and the Christians at the chapel, and say a prayer that my decision was right. They always told me later that it was.

I was kept hectically busy, of course. There was one man I shall never forget who looked suspiciously eager when I offered to do any laundry he might have. He presented me with about thirty shirts – his eyes guiltily avoiding mine as I gasped with shock. It took me three days to iron them!

One night that remains exceptionally vivid was during a period when a man who sometimes had epileptic fits was staying with us. He was very highly strung, and a bit of a hypochondriac. He'd never met people like us before, who showed him so much care and attention, and I think it went to his head.

Fred and I were sound asleep in the middle of the night when through the layers of blissful unconsciousness I became painfully aware that something was waking me up. I heard a stomping sound, and then a loud banging on our door. It was our friend with the fits and the nerves, and something was the matter. He was dying, he informed us at the top of his voice. He had pains and he was dying! And he gave a healthy shriek.

Fred lost his patience. We were exhausted with eight children to raise, long shifts at the local factory; another busy day awaited us. So we told him to die quietly, please.

He stormed around, demanding that we take him to the hospital at once. Anyone who could make such an appalling noise, we reasoned, was quite capable of calling a taxi and going there himself, if he really needed to. He stormed back to his room, and paced back and forth for hours. By the morning he was fine and wanted a big breakfast, which I gave him with a very stern look indeed.

Once we had a drug addict here. She was covered in sores from infected injections. I took one look at her, and one sniff, and told Fred categorically that I wasn't going to have her in the house. She needed professional help in a hospital. Enough is enough!

We had one tragedy with a man named George. He stayed with us for quite a while, but we were careful with him, because we knew he was unstable. But a local girl, Trixi, who went to the Methodist Hall as we did, became friends with him. It happened naturally – she was always around at our house visiting me and helping when the children were young. I noticed that she was coming more and more to see George and not us. She fell in love, against all of Fred's advice. He liked George, but knew him, too: he'd had a string of convictions and was still a badly mixed up person who needed watching.

Trixi wouldn't listen. Her neighbours didn't help by telling her that they thought she and George were the perfect couple. So she married him.

And then he murdered her.

I'd brought the local paper home one day for Fred as usual, and glanced at the headlines before I handed it to him. I saw the name of her housing estate and suddenly had a premonition that something had happened to Trixi. I stumbled out into the garden screaming for Fred. He took the newspaper from my trembling fingers and read the story. George had brutally attacked her while she was asleep – he had smashed in her head with eleven blows from a mallet. He must have been temporarily insane, for he couldn't remember doing it. In fact, they'd often knelt and prayed together. Ten years later he was released from prison, but we didn't have the heart to contact him again.

Usually Fred would bring a fellow home and say, 'Here, take over.' And apart from counselling the man if he wanted it, that, as far as Fred was concerned, would be that – unless I really needed him. Fred ran an open house, and I did a lot of work, but I never grudged him that – if he wanted things done, they were done. I've always let him be head of his own house.

When I look back, I can see the funny side of all those times, and I can laugh until the tears come to my eyes. Just going to church on Sunday morning became a major event – eight children following Fred and me down the road, usually with several hard-bitten, shifty eyed and desperately needy men shuffling in our wake. When we got to the chapel we used to fill nearly half of it!

I don't remember ever minding Fred's hospitality in the least. After all, he did it because it was something he felt he could do for God. I think a woman should encourage her husband to do good works even if it inconveniences her. And though life has got very hectic around here at times, all these people were never a strain on our relationship. Having others around all the time didn't make me feel far from him like it used to. My goodness, the odd people Fred used to bring back home in the early days of our marriage! 'Patience', I would tell myself thirty-five years ago in Barking as I stepped cautiously over the sleeping figure of one of Fred's drunken friends on the floor of our lounge. 'Fred has a right to have friends.'

'Be a good sport,' I told myself the time Fred woke me up well past midnight to tell me he was hungry. Well, not just he ... there were about a dozen others downstairs and they were all agreed that a steak and kidney pudding was just the thing they needed after a couple of hours of beery singing.

'Well, perhaps he's shy,' I told myself the time I went down into our coal cellar and found one of Fred's mates up to his eyes in coal dust. I gave a little scream, and the man came out, making the house filthy. I never did find out what he was doing in there.

I wasn't quite so understanding the night I came home from a visit to my mum's in Peckham and found a crowd of virtual strangers holding a party. I didn't need to unlock the front door – it was wide open with people wandering in and out. Some nodded politely as the children and I struggled inside.

Where was Fred? He wasn't upstairs; I checked as I went with the children to their bedroom. I discovered he wasn't downstairs either! That took a while longer to make sure of, as about fifty other people *were* downstairs, and well and truly crammed in. The party carried on happily as I took myself out to the kitchen in frozen dignity. I wanted to shout: 'Get out, everybody!' I was furious, not at all our guests, but at Fred. That wasn't the first or last time that he started a party at our house and then went down and joined another one at the local pub.

If Fred came in from work and had a cup of tea with me before heading down to the pub, I had to count myself lucky: I'd seen my husband that day! With so many hours alone, I did a lot of thinking. And I decided that Fred's background had not in the least prepared him for marriage. He'd known little or no personal love growing up, and, never knowing his father, had had no opportunity to see parents loving each other. From his earliest years he'd been in institutional schools, where a little fellow like him either survived or he didn't. And the only way out of utter loneliness was to make friends among his peers and earn their respect, value their judgment, strive for their praise.

'Mates' from his childhood on up would never have cared if he was timid or down. To survive at all he had to be tough, even callous. It would never have done to show hurt or admit to weakness.

And Fred certainly had survived his childhood years, and in fact had gone on to spend seven years in the army, most of them getting in trouble for rebelling against authority in one form or another. He was a man's man, through and through. Although he had a love for me, having married me, he wasn't able to adjust and become a family man. I was his wife, but why seek out my company?

I don't think Fred had ever quite realised what marriage would mean to his life. He had never stopped and thought about the responsibilities that go with it. He wasn't ready to give up the freedom of his bachelorhood.

In fact, I could almost say he 'took time off' from his normal life when he fell in love with me and got engaged. All his loyalties and where he felt most comfortable were still with his mates. With them he felt free to do, say and be exactly what he was. He enjoyed the rough and ready company, the carefree men's society.

The circumstances of our engagement made this easy: I was quite a distance away, London was being bombed, so meetings were fairly few and far between. The two different sides of his life never clashed. His love life was firmly removed from the rest of his existence – for even Fred never dreamed of bringing his mates along when he came courting!

So I only met his friends once: we were engaged by then, and he was on leave from the army. Torn between the desire to be with me in Peckham, and the longing not to miss a big party being held near his home in Barking, he'd asked me if I'd like to come along.

I'd said yes. Fred and I shared no friends or common factors in our lives other than Alf and Olive, and I was curious to know more about this man whom I had fallen in love with and was going to marry.

As my experience of parties was that of merry, simple affairs fuelled by fruit punch alone, and enlivened by some light-hearted dancing, I was totally unprepared for what I found that night.

To begin with, as we hurried up the shabby London road at twilight, half of Barking seemed to be trying to get into one particular terraced house. Of course, they didn't all fit. I followed Fred in a state of mild confusion as we struggled through the cheerful throng, up the short path and into the hallway.

People! Men and women everywhere! In the hallway, beyond in the kitchen, in the living room, and even up the staircase in front of me. I was astonished at how loudly they were laughing and talking – far louder than they needed to. But then I was not used to parties where the basis of entertainment was drink.

I felt a bit overwhelmed and determined to stay by Fred's tall, comforting side. That proved harder than I'd thought. I was still getting my bearings when I heard particularly noisy shouts, close at hand. Some of Fred's particularly close mates had apparently just discovered he'd arrived.

I can't remember now whether Fred had a chance to introduce me or not, but I do remember that I spoke hardly a word to anyone that evening. Fred and his mates wanted only each other's company, not mine. That evening, I didn't mind. With the war, they saw each other so seldom, I was content to sit and watch Fred among them, though slightly startled at the amount of booze he was knocking back.

I could see how popular he was, surrounded by other young men. But it was almost like seeing a Fred I'd never met before. I thought about that party a fair bit. My future life certainly seemed as if it would be quite different from what I was used to. I've since wondered if some of their devilment was because of the war – but I doubt it. They were just out for fun.

When you see the man you love only every so often, and he makes casual references to 'me and the mates' it sounds fine. Why shouldn't he have friends, good friends ? Far better to hear that than 'an old girlfriend of mine and I went ... ' Fred was in the army, he had several brothers in Barking; why shouldn't he have mates in both places?

I didn't mind at all. I naturally assumed that when we married, we would go around with them occasionally and that they would visit us. Little did I guess how much they would affect our life! I was to learn that married men came in two varieties: family men and men's men. My father was a family man; Fred was a man's man. And the difference could not have been greater! Fred and his friends never seemed to think that a wife needs some time alone with her husband. Of course, most of Fred's friends were married too, with *their* wives sitting alone at home. It is miserable to sit wondering where your husband is, and how late he's going to be out tonight.

I could never get Fred alone even to argue with him. So many rows seemed to blow up in the kitchen, and immediately spill over in front of other people in the next room. And yet I believed even then, and I have proved it over the years, that it wasn't us who were so incompatible – it was the lifestyles that we had come from.

And I was right. For years now life with Fred has been so very different ... not just because we've helped down and outs together, but because we can now share his friends.

Like the time recently when the telephone rang in our little hallway.

Fred was watching television, I was in the kitchen; I was nearer, so I answered it.

'Hello, Doris,' came a deep hearty voice down the line. 'It's Bill here.' Forty years ago he wouldn't have been so friendly.

I fumbled in the dark for the lightswitch. 'Hello Bill. We haven't heard from you for a while. Must be about two months ... '

'Sure is. How are you? Keeping well?'

Forty years ago he wouldn't have bothered to ask.

'Very well, thank you.'

'When are you both coming down to see us?'

You *both* ... *us*! My goodness, how things change! But then Bill has become a Christian too. 'You'll want Fred. Just a minute, I'll get him.'

I settled comfortably into my chair by the TV and tried to pick up the threads of the programme Fred had been watching. But my mind was still on the phone conversation going on down the hall. Bill. One of Fred's very oldest mates from the days when we lived in East London. I hoped he and Fred could get together sometime soon. Perhaps I'd go along.

Fred's laughter at some joke drifted down the hallway, but it wasn't that that made me smile to myself: it was amusement that the day should have actually come when I'd *want* to see more of Fred's friends ... for now I know he loves me better than them.

11. *Helping your husband to get to heaven*

... we have a building from God, a house not made with hands, eternal in the heavens. 2 Cor. 5:1

It's hard to be a saint. Witness one grey, overcast afternoon in Southampton. Fred and I were occupying our favourite haunts: Fred was blissful in his garden, I was tucked away in the kitchen with a book, keeping an occasional eye on him to make sure he didn't wear himself out.

It was an afternoon he'd looked forward to after a spate of busy days: at last a few hours when he could enjoy some of the peace and tranquillity retirement is supposed to give you. After all, Fred is in his late sixties.

Then I heard voices and saw Fred straighten up slowly and look over towards the street. A rather sorry looking young couple were tentatively coming in the gate. Fred wiped his soiled hands on his trousers and went over to meet them.

'Oh no,' I thought. 'Poor Fred ... '

As usual, he gave them a big welcoming smile, and I heard our front door open and close as he invited them in for a chat in our TV room, which also serves as his study. They were in there for a couple of hours. I guessed it must be a big problem.

When I finished my book, I felt hungry – it was getting on for tea-time. Stretching, I dumped the cat off my lap and went to the fridge. Almost instinctively I thought: now what shall I feed them all?

I rummaged around. Steak. And chips. That would do fine. I scolded a greedy, interested cat off the counter and set to work.

A little while later Fred came to the doorway of the kitchen, looking sober and very abstracted.

'Ah, Doris,' he said, keeping his voice low, and beckoning me to him. 'These people, things are bad for them. They have to go to London, so I'm going to drive them there now. But we should feed them first – just give them anything you've got.'

'Yes,' I said; 'it's ready. Shall I bring it in now?'

His eyes widened in surprise, and at the sight of the steaklets he smiled down at me. 'Great,' was all he said, but the look in his eyes warmed me right through. I had pleased him and I was glad.

Later, as I watched the car pull away from the house, and then still later, five hours or so, as I heard the car park outside again, I felt several conflicting emotions. There was concern for the couple, concern for Fred's fatigue, and regret that he'd lost his day off, but most of all – pride in him. What a husband! To give up a day to strangers like that. And he came in without one complaint, just settling into his chair with a grunt of fatigue, and looking my way. 'What about a cup of tea?'

Gladly, my dear husband who makes such an effort to help people because you believe it is God's work. And gladly will I support you in these things you do because you believe it is God's will for you.

I want to help you.

I hope you don't think the title of this chapter is a bit

presumptuous. Of course I know that only Christ can *really* help people.

I suppose I should really call it: 'Don't make it hard for your husband to live out his Christian life.' After Fred became a Christian, our marriage relationship altered so drastically that I noticed several things that would have been easy to miss had Fred been always more or less a decent person. I noticed a new bent in his will. He wanted to do right, to be kind to other people. His helping down-and-outs and people with problems all came from one fundamental desire: to please God.

So what was *I* doing?

Helping.

This was marvellous! When that dawned on me, I decided then and there to encourage him in every way I could.

If you love your husband and wish him well, why stop at cooking the food he likes, and making a cosy home for you both? Why not concern yourself deeply for his spiritual welfare, and do all in your power to influence him for the good – in whatever form it may take?

I do *not* mean that you should 'preach' at him. Heaven help the poor man whose wife embarks on an extensive cleanup campaign of his personality and habits! I know of no quicker way of ensuring that he will rarely rely on you, turn to you for help, confide in you.

Instead, after you've avoided the temptation to smile up at him with the words 'From now on, darling, I'm going to take a great interest in your spiritual growth' – thus probably frightening him out of his wits – begin with *prayer*.

Spend time with God, and He'll spend time with you. And through the closer acquaintance of the Holy Spirit you'll begin to understand how He sees life. Times with God will also give you a greater sensitivity to other people and their needs – including your husband's needs.

And after prayer?

Well, stop and consider what influence you have on your husband at present. Each of us influences for good or bad those whom we are close to. That is a fact we cannot alter. All we can choose is in what *way* we shall influence them. And I don't mean in great earth-shaking decisions or in constant conversations. I mean in everyday life, by the attitudes with which you approach things, what you believe in and value in life.

Women can have an enormous influence on their husbands, for good or for evil. If you cared enough for your husband to want to marry him, do your best by him now. Tearing him down only hurts you as well in the end; he's your other half.

To me, the fact that Fred wants to preach and tell people about Jesus is marvellous. I think he has all his heart and soul in his preaching and his books. It is his life, and I like the fact that he finds it so absorbing.

So I encourage him. I care about his eternal life, and am willing to stand by him and help him in doing what is good, and to be patient with him. When you add up the environment he grew up in, his life in India, his life in Barking, and Dartmoor and then look at his life today, what a long way he has come! I wouldn't *allow* Fred to go off the straight and narrow way, not now, because I know he is capable of keeping on it. I want to help him by living as close to God as I can, by not being grumbling and bitter. As the Bible says, we show God's love when we love each other. Fred looks to me for encouragement. He is pleased when I praise him, or thank him for anything he has given me. A woman's appreciation and praise means a lot to a man.

The minute Fred had any idea that life was any more

than a battle of wits, and that love and truth really did exist, he responded immediately with all of his heart. I'd rather have him than a thousand of the kind of man who are never very bad, but never very good either, and who live lives of spiritual mediocrity and selfishness. At least my Freddie had the courage to acknowledge the trouble he had got himself into in life. Such a man, straightforward and without guile, deserves total forgiveness and something more: respect.! He certainly arouses and holds my love!

As for my own spiritual life? Well, I'm conscious of God's loving presence all the time. Sometimes I find myself praying and only then realise that I am doing it! I like to read the Bible too – a few years ago I sat down one day and decided to read the entire Bible through, word for word. An ambitious project! It took me a year to read from page one right to the middle before I floundered a bit.

My faith in God is secure, and I know that whatever happens in life, nothing could take that away from me. I know that when Jesus died, He did so that I could find forgiveness for my sins and have eternal life. He has always helped me in many, many ways. And He has given me the wisdom, and the strength, to help Fred where I could. In a way, I think God gave Fred to me all those years ago, so that he would have someone to stand by him all his life and love him.

Since I got stuck in the middle of the Old Testament, I read mostly the New Testament and the Psalms these days. I am especially fond of 1 and 2 Corinthians, and so was glad when we found verses from 1 Corinthians on the posters that we used to hang up when we had the vegetable shop. Then last year Fred was cleaning out the shop and brought home two of these pretty, colourful, delicate posters with birds and Bible verses on them. The first I knew about it was when I went to take a bath. Lo and behold, he had stuck them up on either side of our bathroom window. He'd followed me down the hall and stood in the doorway, admiring his handiwork. 'They look nice there, don't they,' he asked, eyeing them narrowly, making sure they weren't hanging crooked.

I smiled happily. 'Ooh, Fred, they look lovely', I said and felt silly when tears suddenly came to my eyes. I was really touched. Fred's not terribly domestic, and it was a pleasant surprise that he had thought of such a thing. He'd done it all on his own, too.

I reckon my Freddie is going to be okay spiritually. He talks about his faith all the time now – I bet no one will be able to shut him up even when he gets to heaven! And I wonder sometimes how many people he's helped along in the same direction.

12. *No time for the children*

May your father and mother be glad; may she who gave you birth rejoice! Proverbs 23:25

One thing my daughter June inherits from her dad is her strength of personality. When she and her husband Bill drop in for an evening I can be pretty sure that at some point she and Fred will be hotly debating some issue. If her father says a thing is so, it *is* so, and that is that. Only June can be just as adamant the other way. She is her father's daughter!

They argue hammer and tongs: 'No, it isn't,' ... 'Yes, I tell you, it is!', while I watch the clock and hope that 10.30 will hurry up and come. But they take no notice of me, for while I am not fond of a lot of disagreements, they are, and part company feeling great and invigorated. They get along famously, those two, and Fred loves her dearly. As he does Joyce, our second daughter, and John, our son.

When I see them now, all crowded into my sitting room, I'm usually too busy counting heads for tea and catching up on the latest news with a grandchild or two to think of anything else, but every so often it does suddenly strike me that it is, after all, only due to God's grace that any of us are here at all – that after all we've been through, we *are* a family.

I've learned a lot of lessons in my life, but the area of the deepest need for wisdom was raising my children in those early years with a difficult marriage on my hands. How does a woman manage it?

All I can say is, next time you see a woman with a difficult marriage struggling to raise her children with no help from her husband, you may find yourself pitying her. Don't. Those children *may* be the saving of her. Mine were to me.

Oh, I'd have heartily agreed with you if you'd suggested that it would be *nicer* if my husband took an interest in the children (and me!). But if you'd then said 'and of course having the children makes things that much more difficult', I'd have laughed in astonishment. For me, they were precisely what made life worth living for years and years.

My three children were the most marvellous gifts from God that anyone on earth could receive. Over the years they've been my friends, my companions, my comforters ... and now, they are the greatest joy of my old age, and Fred's too.

Even in my early twenties, I was thrilled to bits to discover, a little while after I married Fred, that I was pregnant. I must have been quite an optimistic young lady, because Fred had then just been sent overseas for months with the army to Ireland, and the only place we had to call home was a room in my parent's flat in Peckham. Added to that, London was being blitzed and many nights found my parents and me fleeing to the Old Borough Street tube to join 7,000 other refugees underground. Yet these never seemed to be snags that made pregnancy perhaps not the ideal state for me.

Life was very hard, but it made me long all the more

for that intense private joy of having a baby. I'd been an only child, and had long hated it, and longed for company. In fact, my dearest wish for years and years had been to have brothers and sisters – preferably several, always older. But as the doctor had warned my mother of a risk to her life if she had any more, she stopped. It would in any case have been difficult for her to give me an *older* brother or sister!

So for years I had been very much on my own. I grew up shy, afraid to speak up for myself. At school it was sometimes difficult – the more aggressive children took advantage of me and thought I was a fool not to stand up to them.

Then when I saw my older cousins marry and begin to raise their families, I knew I'd found the solution to my frustrations. I had it all worked out: so far I'd missed out on lots of young company, but when *I* got to be a 'mummy', I was going to really let myself go! 'If I can't have about ten children', I resolved, 'then I just won't have any at all. I won't have just one – I wouldn't inflict that on any child'. Perhaps such 'daydreams' weren't all that extravagant – though I only had three children myself I later adopted five more. God took my early resolve quite seriously!

I loved babies, I delighted in children. When I married, I was going to establish a family – with homely routines, traditions, fun. Next to such blissful determination, what chance had the Second World War of deterring me?

To my delight I'd discovered that Fred liked children too. He was able to get 'leave' and be with me on the day after our daughter June was born. He arrived at the hospital along with his sisters and mother and the very first thing he did was to reach out for me – and knock a large glass brimming with cold water all over me. Those were early days for Fred and I, but I was already beginning to realise I'd married a rough and ready sort! I remember thinking: 'Poor Fred – he can't do anything right!' But still I was so happy. My family was underway.

June was born at a very difficult time. Fred was away in Ireland, and later in France. I never knew when he would turn up, or how to contact him. I had fairly frequent letters, but they were little more than hastily scribbled notes. I was very lonely for him.

So June filled a gap for me. And I had my mum to help me – though that was a mixed blessing as she wanted to take over everything to do with June, and got very angry when I wanted to do things for myself! Mum really was dotty about June.

Nevertheless, I didn't want to impose on her for a home. I found a flat nearby, four flights up in a huge old house, which was all boarded up downstairs. The landlord said I could have it for ten shillings a week, and he set about taking down the board covering my windows. I was there for a considerable time before Fred even knew I'd left my mother!

The flat was near my parents, and when the air raid sirens went, they used to dash over and up my several flights of stairs, and we'd all run for our lives into the dug out. At one period there was an air raid every night. Dad would have to return home afterwards because of his work the next day, but mum would spend the night with me. And if we listened to the radio, we could tell when another raid was coming – it would begin to crackle.

Joyce arrived two years after June, in a London that was being fiercely bombed. Fred used to worry when he left me after a 'leave' that he would never see me again. By now mum and dad and I used a local shelter and not the tube, so we no longer faced certain drowing if the bombs ever hit the flood gates beside the tube entrance.

Things between Fred and me had been good but at the time of Joyce's birth I was thinking of leaving him. We'd had a frightful row before he'd gone back to Ireland, and I had even sent my paybook back to the army, with a curt note to say that I was finished with my husband. This brought several officers round to my parents in a great hurry, to try to get me to change my mind.

They pleaded for Fred very well but I didn't believe all those messages he'd sent as to how sorry he was. He'd say anything at a time like this – but when it came to living with him ... ! So I remained angry and aloof.

Joyce arrived a week after that – she was nearly born in our garden where I was planting peas one twilight evening. Fortunately the ambulance came quickly, for she came very shortly after the first warning!

Mum and Dad were thrilled. 'But how will you manage *two* children?' Mum inquired. 'June's a job in herself to take on.'

I smiled, a bit weakly. 'Well, you're going to have to look after one, and I'll look after the other.'

That delighted her, and it was only as an afterthought that she added, as they left for the night, 'Has anyone notified Fred?'

'No,' I said coolly. 'Why should I?'

A loaded question. She blinked. 'Well, I think you ought to,' she said. Of course she was right, but still I never did. It was a week or so before Fred found out through my mum.

Because it was months before we had sorted out the matter of my sending back his pay, I went out to work as soon as I could after Joyce's birth. Mum took care of the two little girls while I worked part-time in a gas mask factory, packing the hideous things into large cardboard boxes. I earned enough to support myself and the girls and keep our little flat going.

It was hardly an auspicious beginning to the cosy family I had longed for, but Fred and I eventually made up, so things could have been worse. They were by the time John arrived, another two years later; for Fred had been in prison for three weeks, just beginning his first sentence of two years for robbery.

Two weeks before, I had visited Fred in prison and had brought him cigarettes and other items he had asked for. I gave them to him as he'd requested, while he was out in the exercise yard, and I didn't know there was anything wrong by being so close to the fence and passing things over to Fred until a guard suddenly shouted and started towards us. Fred jumped back and cried: 'Quick! Get out of it! Run!' and in a panic I stumbled off across towards the canal, terrified. The guard didn't catch me – possibly because I chose the highly dangerous method of crossing the canal by leaping across the logs that were floating there. Two weeks later John was born, a bit early. I might well have miscarried and lost him in such a mad scamper. My mother came to look after the two little girls and Fred never even saw John until he was two years old. From the beginning I always, I'm sorry to say, felt the children were more mine than his.

One suggestion I would make to any woman with a difficult marriage is this: if there are children, do try and live as peaceably with your husband as you can. And if you can't, do hide as much as you possibly can from them. It may be very difficult, pretending you're cheerful when you're miserable, but you'll see your reward daily in the untouched faces of your children.

If parents can't solve their own problems but must

start piling them on the shoulders of youngsters, then I think it is a pretty poor show. Children need as good a start as possible in life. They should not have to listen to their parents fighting all the time. Worrying about adult problems they cannot understand will only damage them. It's not the duty of a child to solve an adult's problems.

Well I remember one particular autumnal night in Barking when after a terrific row Fred pushed me right out of the house, and locked the door on me, leaving me in my thin dress out on the street late at night. I pounded and pounded on the door, until I realised with horror that he'd gone off to bed. My children were asleep in there! They might call me! In desperation I went around back to the kitchen window and banged in a pane of glass with my shoe. I climbed awkwardly through the window and succeeded in slicing up my arm, leaving a scar that is there today.

Then I discovered Fred's coup de grace: *he'd locked the kitchen door.* Had he guessed I would come in that way? Rather than scream the house down and probably give the children the fright of their lives, I decided I'd just stay in the kitchen and wait until morning. It was freezing with the window gone, so I crept under the kitchen table and lay down and tried to go to sleep. As I shifted about uncomfortably on the hard floor I felt my dress and arms and legs being scratched – I'd been lying on broken glass.

Early in the morning Fred's brother arrived at our front door and let himself into the house with a key. He was astonished to open the kitchen door and find me lying on the floor inside, all scratched and a bit bloody and more than close to tears. He let me out and we listened to see if Fred had woken up. He hadn't, so I crept into the bedroom, grabbed some clothes to cover my cuts, and went to the bathroom to wash and change. Fred's brother bandaged my arm, and even apologised a bit on Fred's behalf. Then I practised a cheerful smile in front of the bathroom mirror. In the cold early morning light I admit the most I could produce was a ghastly smirk, but I wore it anyway, and when the children woke up shortly after that, they didn't even know anything had gone wrong, though they were fascinated by the hole in our kitchen window and mummy's apparent indifference as to how it got there.

You may have a difficult husband, but don't go out of your way to discuss him with your children. If you have a serious problem with him then it is the kind of thing that you should take to a trusted friend or counsellor to deal with, or perhaps just to God. After all, *you* married the man, so the problem is now yours. I believe you may do greater harm than you know if you turn to the children for comfort.

Why? Because they can't handle it. Their first and earliest trust and love is in you, their mother. If their earliest knowledge of Daddy is that he is that big man who is hurting you and causing you distress, you may have destroyed forever any chance of their loving their daddy with childish abandon. You may feel better for having aired your woes, and may go on to forgive and mend things with your husband. But what may be a rough year or two in your marriage becomes embedded in their young minds as Reality.

We've all heard stories of how mothers can frighten their children off snakes and mice and climbing trees and many other things, for a child will adopt your attitudes to things when it is very young. A child can live without a close relationship with a snake or a mouse (and it is probably better off without them!) but not without its father.

And what about your husband? If he knows he is now the 'bad guy' not only to you but to the kids as well, it won't make life easier for him either.

So no matter what a man's done to his wife, it seems to me cruel for her to get back at him by alienating the children. She is rarely, if ever, entirely in the right (I certainly wasn't! I had lots of irritating ways) and they are after all, his children too.

I'm not denying that your husband may be a wicked man, but at least give him a chance to be good with children. The sad thing, of course, is that if he is so awful with you, he may be evil to the children as well. What then?

If a woman is faced with a choice between staying with a man who is harming the children, or going – well, I know I'd go.

For years I stayed with Fred only because the children needed a father; but I'd have left him finally, not because our marriage was totally impossible for me, but because of the kind of father he was.

After all, he could be quite callous towards them. Once he was sprawled in front of a wood fire and little June came along and tried to get by. He watched her indifferently, and made no effort to move his legs out of the way. So she got too close to the fire in trying to get by. In fact, she caught the heat so badly on her legs and bottom that her skin peeled off in ugly blisters. I was furious with him, but kept still as I bandaged her, for fear I would get hysterical. I wanted to kill him that night. June was only just starting school, but nearly forty years later she still remembers that incident.

On the whole, fortunately, June and Joyce and later John were mainly indifferent to Fred. They rarely saw him and had little to do with him. They used to play whether he was around or not, and he never did anything with them anyway.

120

I don't know whether the children realised about all the drinking, but Fred certainly never harmed the children when drunk – though I was scared stiff that he would, and used to keep them well out of his way. In fact, his drinking made me furious precisely on account of the children – and especially during the war years, when money was so short. How could Fred and his mates spend what they had on drink and not on the children?

Several times our pantry ran out of food. When I went to Fred about it, he'd give me a few bob, and so we carried on.

I worked for a time when we lived in Barking, so as to help Fred with household finances. Then I came home one night to find June and Joyce sitting in front of the open fire, not properly dressed, and a pot between them with a lump of hard and greasy steak in it. I was furious. Fred was happy for me to go out to work, but he wasn't keeping his side of the bargain in feeding the children properly when he got in.

Soon after that I hurt my foot in a snowy street and left work. Why bother to struggle up to Tower Bridge and back each day if he didn't even appreciate it? I didn't return to work until some time after – when I found a creche where I could leave June and Joyce safely.

Of course, I couldn't hide the fact that Daddy was rarely around, and that there were sometimes more than seventy people in the lounge, all drinking heavily and carrying on noisily, and even sometimes fighting up and down the street. But I made up my mind not to moan about it. Instead, I pretended to accept it without any fuss for as long as the children were around. And so, of course, they accepted it too. How were they to know any different? For much of those years they were still so young that they hardly understood what was going on.

The main thing to them was that I was always there, for them to turn to; I was interested in the little goings on in their small lives.

Fred ignored them, but then he always had, and it didn't bother them because I never told them that Daddy should be loving them. What they thought were lovely long bus rides over to Peckham to visit Grandma were really me at my breaking point with Fred, when I couldn't stand it a minute longer. I'd wrap up little John in a shawl, gather some food for the four of us (Mum wasn't well off, either) and off we'd go, for a day, for even a week at a time. We were back and forth like yo-yo's at one point, but it didn't disturb the children because they associated no distress with the journeys, and loved their granny. It was a nice outing for them, and a much needed breathing space for me. Children are amazingly adaptable. They can easily accept what goes on around them as long as they feel secure and cared for.

Although I may have had very little materially to give them, I could give them something. I believed that the most valuable thing to pass on to my children was not material goods, but ideas, values with which to deal with whatever they had to face in life. For me, this meant teaching them the Christian faith. For I believed devoutly in God. I'd been raised a 'Christian girl' and I was determined to do the same by them. Fred's main problem, I felt, wasn't drinking, or wildness, or tempers; it was his total disregard for any of God's laws.

My dearest wish for my children was not that they would become rich and get ahead in life, but that their whole motivation in life would be different. For I had, in the early years, a niggling fear that they would grow up to be like Fred. For my children to turn to drink and crime ... I don't think I could have borne it.

So I took measures against it: I was going to bring

them up as Christians. When they were little I told them a bit about what I knew of God whenever it seemed suitable. I taught them to pray and I prayed with them each night. They were soon saying prayers of their own, except for little Johnnie, who was such a little tiddler that I whispered along with him, resisting the desire to hug that dear little three-year-old scrap to me in love at the expression on his face.

When I first found out that Fred was involved in illegal activities, I nearly left home at once. If Fred wanted to get in trouble, that was his business, but I wasn't going to have that stigma on my children. Yet I never wanted to tell the police about Fred, because of the children. I couldn't bring trouble on my own family.

When Fred was sent off to Dartmoor, and I returned from my nine months sentence in Askham Grange, I had the raising of the children to myself – and a very peaceful existence it was too! We fell into a daily routine very quickly: I walked the children to school in the morning, back for lunch, back for their afternoon lessons, and then home again in the late afternoon. The only part I did regret was that the children hardly knew Fred – certainly little John had rarely had a Daddy around.

It was lonely sometimes. With the children in from school, we shut ourselves in for the evening. Except for Frances.

I met her at the British Legion which I'd found was fairly near our home. When I first found it, I had no idea what it was, but I went in anyway and asked if they ever took church services. The man at the reception looked slightly startled. 'Yes, why?' he asked.

'Well,' I said, 'I have three children, and I am on my own, and I want to do the right thing for them as regards their worship.'

'Oh,' he said, looking only a little less confused. 'Well, this is the right place, bring them here.'

So – we went to British Legion's services! I was satisfied, although I could afford to put only about three old pennies in the money box at any service. But the main thing was for the children to have some training. The fact that I was satisfied with the British Legion and didn't look for a lively Church fellowship only shows how little I actually knew in those days. I had a faith in God but I didn't know you could have a personal relationship with Him.

And then we met Frances. She stopped me one day as I was going out of the British Legion's front door. 'I seem to know your face,' she began abruptly. 'Weren't you in the papers?'

'Yes,' I said, and then dried up. I didn't want any more gossip about Fred and me to go around the neighbourhood.

'Well, how are you getting on? I'd heard your husband was away. You are Fred Lemon's wife, aren't you?'

I was stung by her abruptness. 'Yes,' I said, 'That's right. Why, are you going to ignore me now, and turn your head away when I come by?' I knew I sounded bitter, but I felt bitter! I'd been hurt so much, I was very sensitive to how people acted towards me.

'Oh no,' she laughed. 'I'm glad to have met you. I'll tell you what, I'll come around to your house one night each week if you like and give your children Bible lessons. For free, of course. It'll help you out.' She smiled cheerfully.

I was astonished. 'Oh no,' I said. 'I can't put you to all that trouble!'

'No trouble at all, I'd love to do it.'

So Frances came, and told them Bible stories once a week the whole time that Fred was away. She never missed once. And if she saw me out in the road during the day, she'd wave cheerily and cry: 'Hello Doris!' – no matter who saw her. Everyone in Barking knew I was Fred Lemon's wife and not all of them were happy to speak to me after he was sent away to Dartmoor.

I was very fortunate as the children grew older: I was able to enrol them in a good, local Church school. The headmaster was so kind: by this time I found life very tough going financially, so he sent me chits so that I could buy my three school uniforms. They had a good education there, including some religious instruction. John certainly developed an acute appreciation of God's creation: he started collecting spiders and other creepy crawlies in matchboxes at one point – to the teacher's and my own distress! He also loved God's good earth, and got far too interested in a newly tarred piece of it once in the schoolyard – cleaning him up drove us all to our wits' end!

When we moved to Southampton and met up with Fred again, I was careful for a long time not to tell them where Daddy had been. I simply said that he had been away and was now coming back again. So they were pleased to see him, and had no upsets about it at all. It took them a bit of time to get to know Fred again – and though there were tremendous changes in him, they hardly noticed – they'd been too young when he was sent away.

Then, just as we were settling nicely in Southampton, I was contacted by a lady from the West Ham Council, in London. She was from a children's home where, it turned out, Fred's five nephews and nieces had been placed when his sister, for various reasons, was unable to care for them. She wanted to come to Southampton to talk to me; did I mind? I told her to come right along, with no inkling of what was coming.

When she arrived she asked me what I thought were

some rather strange questions: was I thinking of having any more children? were we settled now in Southampton?

Yes, we were settled in Southampton, I replied, and no, I wasn't going to have any more children. Whereupon she looked very pleased and leaned forward.

'Mrs Lemon,' she said, and smiled.

'Yes?'

'Mrs Lemon,' she said again. 'I wonder. Would you be willing to take those children?'

'What!' both Fred and I exclaimed together.

It seemed that the home was closing down and as Fred's sister was unable to take them back, if we did not give them a home, they would be split up and sent to different places.

She next took me up to London to meet the children. I looked down at them, at teenage Michael, at nine-year-old Patricia, seven-year-old Tom, three-year-old Sylvia and two-year-old David. They stared up at me solemnly and I was lost.

Fred and I held a council of war. We had three bedrooms. If we did some more shifts at the factory in the evening we could just about afford it. We had no choice – we just couldn't desert those poor children. I had some moments of doubt after we'd said yes, fearing the strain it would put on Fred.

'That's all right, love,' he said. 'You've done the right thing. I'm behind you every inch of the way.'

So I thanked God and felt very relieved!

Near Christmas the ladies brought them down. Fred sat down in his chair and was immediately buried under a mass of kids. He eventually emerged and grinned at me: we'd done it now. We were the legal parents of eight children.

They were a lively little mob, and we were fortunate in that our three didn't mind the sudden population explosion. They quite happily accepted their cousins as a part of the Lemon family.

Fred coped with the children very well. He'd play with them at night while I got the dinner ready. Sometime he looked a bit like Father Christmas – knee deep in children! I kept them amused in other ways. We had a field behind our house where a motorway runs now, and I would send them black berry picking there. I'd hand out bags to put the blackberries in – the bigger the child, the bigger the bag!

Those eight children I considered to be sent straight from God, if via the West Ham Council. Somebody had to take them, and God sent them to me. Who else would have accepted five extra members in their family at a few weeks notice?

The five all had such different temperaments. David was a whiner and Sylvia could be a little spitfire: when she was three she picked up a bucket I'd left at the top of the stairs and hurled it down at me with all her strength. Patricia, a little older, was better behaved, which helped in some measure to make up for Tony, who was the naughtiest of the lot and even stole from the church before he was ten. My three were much better to deal with, but then at least they'd had me to love and provide security for them. But I went ahead and treated those five as if they were mine as well. I felt sorry for them – they'd had such a bad start in life. They needed a real home, with real parents!

Fred was marvellous. He took them to his heart and really loved them. I was very proud if him – there are very few men who would adopt five children soon after returning from prison! But he had a good heart, especially where children were concerned.

Of course, it meant that Fred and I had very little time alone together. But because it was the children that kept us busy and not his drinking and mates, the hectic life didn't harm our marriage. We took them round to all the local sights as much as we could, and played games with them. People used to smile when they saw our troupe approaching – we took up a good portion of any pavement!

We had some laughs! When they were very young, Fred was on night work and I was on evening shift, to help him out financially. Just before I left for work each night, I'd put them all to bed. In the beginning I hit a snag: how could I say prayers with all this lot? So we finished up by saying the Lord's prayer out loud together every night. I'd stand in the middle of the passage and start them off, and woe betide the little voice I never heard!

When we moved to the house where we live now, the extra corner in the lounge downstairs gave me an opportunity to make it into a 'holy room'. God had done so much for our family, and I wanted the children to grow up with a live Christian faith. So we used to meet there to sing choruses and pray together. The children loved it. With eight children and a steady stream of men in need passing through, the house got rather crowded at one point. So Fred and John took it into their heads to relocate the staircase, knock down a wall in the living room, and put in an extra room downstairs.

I knew they had this planned, but was still rather stunned to come home one evening just before Christmas and find them hard at it with mallets and drills and hammers. What a mess! We ate our Christmas dinner that year amongst the sawdust.

After that the 'Holy Room' really could come into its own. We kept it as a niche in the house where anyone could go for a chat or a pray. I used to get all children to sit on the floor in there and we'd have a mini gospel evening. And then I'd remove them one by one for their Friday night bath – we had a big fire going in the kitchen stove, heating the water. Eight children! I don't think I could do it again.

I would never have forced the children to be religious in any way whatever. I think that if a child isn't interested, the most you should do is to talk with him and encourage him. Soon after our arrival in South-ampton, Fred got it into his head that his children should know more about the Bible. So every time he and I had to go out anywhere and leave the children behind, he set them a passage of the Bible to learn by heart by the time we returned. 'Or I'll give you a hiding!' he'd add menacingly. (He was still a young Christian and his enthusiasms went a bit overboard at times.)

I used to worry as we left the house – suppose June and Joyce and John, looking up at us so soberly, could not remember their verses? But they always did – and as I sat nervously, still in my hat and coat, while they recited to Fred, I'd be afraid to say anything, but breathe a great sigh of relief when all went well.

This system of Bible learning went along well for ages, and as well as helping the children learn a bit about the Bible, kept them inside and off the streets, for we were afraid of the traffic. Even Fred was amazed and impressed by them – until a certain afternoon ...

He and I were returning home and as we reached a street near our house I suddenly saw my three children ahead. Joyce was parading about in my best dress (which Fred and I had saved up to get so I wouldn't have to go the Central Hall in my overall) and as the hem was far too long for her, she'd stepped on it and torn the dress. John stood nearby, pretending to smoke away on a bit of rolled paper. Fred gave a yell and sprang forward, to the children's dismay. Joyce and John were caught and given a hiding there and then, but June was too fast for her father and stayed well away from the house until our tempers cooled down. I smiled ruefully to myself as I cooked dinner that night. They could recite bits and pieces of the Bible like little angels, but I somehow felt that the general message hadn't greatly sunk in as yet!

The children liked going to church in Southampton, and their friends wanted to come along as well. When June and Joyce were teenagers, June's lovesick boyfriends used to trail along. We had quite an impressive little procession.

As for today – well, thanks to God, June and Joyce and John are happily married with kids of their own and everybody seems to be fairly well adjusted to life. They seem to have survived all those early traumas without too many scars – though I still notice, even now, that June is very protective towards Joyce and John.

The children know, as I have always done, that they should forgive Fred for any lingering bad memories that they have of him. Fred, after all, has had hard lessons to learn. Fred made a big difference to our children's childhood, but God has made an even bigger difference to their life as whole. He gave me wisdom in raising them, and giving them a code of life to live by.

The children have probably meant more to Fred over the years than he is willing to say. As for my early worries that they would turn out like him, they do have hot tempers and strong wills, but they are not remotely hard or callous, as he once was. Even John, now a father of three, is bringing his children up superbly. June runs a private nursing home for children and takes after her dad in that she loves people.

130

My grandchildren have been the light of my life since they were born. Many a time I have walked through Southampton when they were toddlers, with all five holding on to me, while June and Joyce strolled along behind, catching up on news. June and I are very close – it sometimes seems I can't move without her wanting to know where I am. Joyce keeps in very close contact as well. They've both turned out so well. I don't think I could have managed without them.

13. *My rough diamond*

She brings him good, not harm, all the days of her life.
Proverbs 31:12

'A long time ago I came home from over the seas and met a beautiful young girl – and that was your mum.'

That was how Fred used to tell our children the story of how our family had begun. Little June, Joyce and John, sitting on his lap or on the edge of the chair, would be tickled to death, not just at the attention they were getting from Daddy, but also at the idea of Mum and Dad ever being young enough to fall in love.

Yet we were young once, and we did fall in love! And though I married a rough diamond, my marriage has turned out the way my father once said that it could: 'Good can come out of evil, my girl, but you must have faith in God.'

When I first began thinking of writing about my marriage, one of the biggest things that struck me was my deep love for Fred. I'd be lost without his warm self in bed beside me at night, and without him as a part of our homely family routine. He often holds my hand in company, but if he forgets, I slide mine into his. He always takes my hand when we cross roads, because the traffic makes me nervous. And then there are the frequent kisses I get. Fred has a sort of rule that it is not really proper for me to come in or go out of the house without a kiss. Even if I've just come back from the shops to drop off some shopping and have to go back again because I've forgotten something, I still get a kiss in between. And he never goes off anywhere to preach without inviting me to come along, asking me again if I'm *sure* I don't want to come along, kissing me good bye, and ringing me from wherever he's gone if he's preaching some distance away and has arranged to stay for the night.

Fred knows very well that I love him, and I think he really loves me too. At least once a day he puts his two great arms around me and hugs me. It's like being held by a bear – he is so enormous compared to me! He tries to please me in many homely ways; still calling me by his favourite nickname since our courtship first began: his 'Dorothy Lamour' girl. And lately, since our retirement, Fred's started taking me out to dinner one day a week. He wants to treat me, and I don't offer to pay.

There's not a thing I wouldn't do for Fred. I take a pride in doing his shirts and shoes for him. Fred is a rough and ready dresser at times and I'm sometimes a bit afraid that if he took it into his head to go to a big meeting in his jumper and patched trousers, he would! He is not self-conscious, and has little interest in his appearance. He has never tried to put on airs, and is happy to be working class. After all, he isn't there to please people, but God. As for his cap, I'm sure sometimes he must have glued it to his head – he wears it constantly.

People don't laugh at Fred for being a Cockney, because his sincerity comes across. The way he tells people what God has done for him and can do for them is so convincing. I'm used to hearing him give his testimony by now – though I can remember that when he first started speaking a lot, I cringed inside and felt very nervous because I knew he was nervous.

I was also embarrassed that he told all these crowds of people how awful he had been. I would rather have tried to forget those years and lived a normal, quiet life in Southampton. Nowadays I'm used to his preaching, but still find the reception that we are given a bit overwhelming. All these people I've never met in my life come up and hug me! Being shy, I've never felt tempted to put on airs because of all the fuss. I just give the women a hand with the cooking and leave it at that. Fred commands the attention and that is just how I want it.

I've never been asked to 'speak', in fact just the thought quite terrifies me. I was called on to the stage at the Filey convention once, in front of all those bright lights. I thought they just wanted me up there to sit with Fred, and with 4,000 people in the place, that made me nervous enough. But then the compère for the evening suddenly produced a microphone and put it in front of me and asked me a question. I couldn't answer – I was so stunned that I hadn't even heard or understood what he'd said. The auditorium was pitch black, except for the row of white faces in the front row, just beyond the blazing lights, and I was terrified. I finally muttered something. Fred was very understanding about it afterwards – he's never tried to get me to do any public speaking.

Two of the best trips Fred ever took me on were to quite different places from Filey; one was to visit a prison in the north of England, and the other was to a prison in Germany. After Fred spoke we had a chance to mingle with the lads that had come to hear him, and they clustered around me as well. I felt quite comfortable and natural and was happy to chat with them. Some of them were so miserable, and so appreciative of any visitors. Soon they would be out on the streets again, and in need of a home and some loving care as they found their feet in the world – just like the dozens of men whom Fred and I have taken in over the years. We stayed there nearly all day, talking to them about God.

Even in the days when Fred was still running our vegetable shop, his desire to tell people about God was just as keen. In fact, it was almost a case of 'if the evangelist can't get to the meeting to address people, let the people come to the evangelist'! I've sometimes wondered whether we ran a vegetable shop that offered prayers and counselling or a counselling organisation that sold vegetables on the side. People will sometimes approach someone in their street, who doesn't seem any different from them, rather than seek out the local vicarage or manse and make an appointment to see a minister who dresses neatly, speaks well, and invites them into his office.

On the days I was helping Fred at the shop, he could take time off to talk to people. Sometimes he'd end up praying outside with them for up to half an hour. It was seen to be a 'Christian' shop as we always had lots of posters with Bible texts up on the wall. After my own retirement, when I worked more and more in the shop with Fred, I noticed that everybody who came in would read the texts. After a few weeks my customers soon passed from being just a mass of people in pursuit of turnips or potatoes or a half pound of tomatoes to being individuals, some of whom needed help.

They used to tell me their problems, for I enjoyed chatting too, and no matter how busy I was, I always made sure I had time for each one. You'd be surprised at what you can learn about people working in a vegetable shop! For me, the Christian help we were able to give people was the main reason for us being there at all.

Our shop had four rows of shelves, with a big bench and some boxes behind that. Near the window by the door we kept a container with lots of texts so that anyone who wanted one would help themselves, in case we should be too busy. Often the housewives would come in, collect some texts, smile cheerily and say: Hello – I'll be back in the morning for my veg!'

I was always careful to be friendly and civil at the shop, no matter how tired I felt. Fred and I may have been the only Christians that some of our customers knew, and I wanted to be a good example. They are very few Christian bookshops in the Southampton area.

I've looked to God over the years to protect me and give me strength and I'm sure He did it with regard to that shop as well. I would often take it on by myself while Fred went off preaching. He would always try to get me to come along, but I felt that if I went around with him it was time wasted when I could have been spending it in the shop. I worked like a Trojan hauling vegetables around all day, and then went home to housework, but I felt no bad effects at all. Sometimes I had two women each wanting a large bag of potatoes – that was a bit much, so I used to say, 'Half a minute – I've got mates outside who'll help me'. Then I would go outside and stop the first young man who came down the pavement. I'd say: 'Excuse me, would you do a "girl guides" for me?' and I got their help every time!

I loved my work in that shop and made a lot of friends through it. I meet them in the street now often. People have stopped both Fred and me and told us how they miss those Bible texts, and how they miss the cheery smile of Mrs Lemon! And I get a lump in my throat and remember how kind they were.

One thing that writing this book has done for me is that I've had to evaluate my marriage. These past years have been so happy, so peaceful, that I hadn't really sat down and thought things out.

We had a young, romantic, idealistic love for each other when we married. It soon went. And that kind of romantic, 'falling in love' experience never comes back once it has been lost.

I've never had the feeling of falling in love with him again. I think the world of him, and I do love him, but it is not in the same way, not like my first, intense love. But since those early years of my youthful, bridal love for Fred, my love has grown up to my present mature, and gently workaday love, based on knowledge, tolerance, and a great deal of humour, plus simple enjoyment of each other's company. No longer is it based, as it was when I first fell in love, on expectation but little knowledge.

The tragedy of so many marriages today is that young people go into them expecting so much, but finding so very little. They don't know what love is, but they do know they haven't found it where they had hoped to.

If you can realise that perhaps your bad marriage is only a symptom of an entire life in a mess – without God – then it is hard medicine, but ultimately the only cure for you. God loves you, He wants to heal you, He wants your marriage to survive.

Perhaps when 'troubles' come in a marriage, it is not 'trouble' breaking in, but reality. Without God, we are not meant to find happiness: no marriage can give you the satisfaction that comes from a relationship to God. It is only when we put Him first, when we don't make everything depend on a happy marriage, that we are at last prepared for married happiness here on earth.

God needs to be in every marriage. Good marriages

are only good because they include the Christ-like qualities of love, trust, consideration, faithfulness and unselfishness.

You may say, 'It's easy for you to talk about making a marriage work: Your husband is a Christian – mine isn't'. Well, for years and years, Fred wasn't! And through those years I learned about patience, forgiveness, endurance. I see now that God was at work in those hard years – they were evil, but giving them over to God strengthened me rather than destroyed me. God can use even the bad things in life to build our characters.

None of us knows how much inner strength and resources we have. Life brings them out – and more important, life puts them into you. You can't choose what will come your way, but you can either let circumstances strengthen you or embitter and destroy you. Self-pity will destroy you quicker than anything else; there's no gain in walking around as though you were the victim of a great tragedy.

Of course, you may *be* the victim of a great tragedy, but in that case let others mourn your plight; the proper business for you is to set about your cure. I'm not saying you shouldn't ever feel sad – but don't give way to self pity. It will never heal your hurts. You must seek God – He promises to bind up the broken hearted.

That's the way I've learned to deal with heartache. It took me years. I had to learn the hard way. Nowadays I take my hurts to God and don't let bitterness poison my entire life.

If you can reach old age and with your faith in God and your sense of humour in tact, I reckon you've had a pretty successful life.

God gave me my sense of humour (it must have come from somewhere!) and it has been a real help. I love life, and I always have. I love my grandchildren, the sight of Fred in his garden; I look back and feel quite content at the life I have lived. I've had nothing to complain about compared with many people!

I found my fulfillment when I found Fred. I've never wanted any other man. Never. Even though he hasn't always given me the love I've wanted from him, I still wanted only him. Yes, he's a rough diamond, but a diamond still. And as everyone knows, diamonds, however rough, are forever!

Other Marshalls Paperbacks

BETRAYED

Stan Telchin

Betrayed! That was the stunned reaction of Stan Telchin, a successful Jewish businessman, when his daughter Judy rang him up to say that she had accepted Jesus as her Messiah.

Stan was shocked by Judy's new commitment, regarding it as a betrayal of their family, their race, their heritage. Grimly, he decided to prove to Judy how wrong she was, and so re-unite the family. He began an angry quest which went on for weeks, then months. In searching through the Bible he not only came to understand what it meant to be a Christian, but what it really meant to be a Jew, and, finally, what Jesus Christ means to all men and women. At the end of his quest, he finds that the rest of his family have all been on the same path . . .

This true story rings with the excitement of prophecy fulfilled in our day. It is full of fascinating insights into how Jesus was regarded by the Jews of his time, and how they see Him now. It is about a whole family's search for true faith and the healing of seemingly irreparable division.

WITH GOD MY HELPER

Ruth Sanford

A Christian woman shouldn't be satisfied with simply 'getting through' her day.

God wants you to do more than just survive—he planned your life to be rich and rewarding. He wants you to have victory over your daily struggles, and he wants you to be respected and honoured.

Many women believe this truth, but don't know how to make it a reality in their lives. Ruth Sanford shares how women can overcome common personal problems such as anxiety, guilt, discouragement, bitterness, and a poor self-image, to experience the full joy and contentment of being a Christian woman.

WHERE CHRIST IS STILL TORTURED

Richard Wurmbrand

'Except for the Bible, nothing has shaken me like Wurmbrand.' *Tortured for Christ*. 'It is the message of the century—Even more: it is the most powerful *Acts of the Martyrs* since the persecution of Christians by Nero.'

Kurt Koch

In this book Richard Wurmbrand brings the story up to date. Persecution continues to tighten its grip on infant Christian Churches in lands ruled by atheists and tyrants. It is only the power of the Holy Spirit which enables them to survive and flourish in the face of discrimination, oppression, torture and murder. What is the response of the cossetted Western church? Does it understand what is happening? Satanic forces are working to stifle Christian witness in the world today, and Christians in the West need to be able to recognize and fight their enemy.

POPE OR GOSPEL?

David Samuel

Is the Reformation still relevant? Can Protestants now welcome the Pope, and prepare for the coming great Church of the future? These questions urgently require an answer.

In this book the differences between Roman Catholicism and Protestantism are clearly stated. But, more than that, the spirit and orientation of the two systems are compared in such a way as to show that the divide goes much deeper than is commonly supposed.

The author argues that Protestantism is not merely a negative critique of the Church of Rome, but is primarily a powerful testimony to the Biblical Gospel. If Protestantism dies the Church dies, and the neglect of Reformation teaching today can only mean that the Church is in imminent danger. The message of Protestantism is needed today both by the Church and society to restore and maintain spiritual, moral and political values. This book will help Protestants to gain a fresh appraisal both of Roman Catholicism and of their own faith.

THE PRACTICE OF BIBLICAL MEDITATION

Campbell McAlpine

Did you know that the Bible recommends meditation?

Meditation can bring you peace of mind and strengthen your faith. It is a divinely approved way of coming closer to God. But there is a right way and a wrong way. This book gives you the lessons which the Bible writers learnt and the methods they recommend. It gives you day to day instructions on how you can meditate and find inner security. It measures the results you can obtain.

Biblical meditation will transform your life. Learn it, practice it, preach it.

BREAKTHROUGH

Fred Lemon

Since his 'amazing encounter' with Jesus Christ in a Dartmoor prison cell Fred Lemon has tried to live uncompromisingly by God's standards rather than the world's. In this book he tells of what God has been saying and doing in many situations since then, of strangers and friends who have been helped, saved or lost. Here we see real-life illustrations of—

—how God deals with people
  answers to prayer
  praising God in times of difficulty
  God's healing power
  how Christians should live
  how God provides for our daily needs—

LOVE IN 'BOMB CITY'

Ben Forde with Chris Spencer

Ben Forde, a Belfast CID detective, shares from his personal experience his conviction that amid the sectarian hatred there is a powerful force of love at work—a love which is bringing forgiveness and healing in a province notorious for its bitterness and division.

He also discusses Northern Ireland from the wider perspective of God's sovereign plan, seeking to make sense of the suffering with which he comes into contact almost every day in the course of his work. He asks: Has God forsaken Northern Ireland? Is he passing judgment on the sins of the people? Or is he actively preparing Ulster for a specific role in future world events? And what of the terrorism? Will the troubles in Northern Ireland ever end? What is the real purpose behind the violence? And how can countries like Britain and America, where terrorism is only just beginning to rear its ugly head, benefit from the painful experiences of Northern Ireland?

Love in 'Bomb City' provides some stimulating answers.

WITH A CHURCH LIKE THIS WHO NEEDS SATAN?

Clive Calver

Beware—Satan is at large in the Church of Britain today and he is using you to do his work for him!

Clive Calver declares it is time to stand aside and look to God to restore our sense of urgency and compassion, to give us a new vision and a new hope. It is time to regain faith in ourselves, in those around us, and in the God who is waiting to achieve through us all that he has promised. To fulfil our true potential as sons of God and heirs to heaven.